SPIRITUAL DIRECTOR, SPIRITUAL COMPANION

Guide to Tending the Soul

TILDEN EDWARDS

 · PAULIST PRESS · NEW YORK / MAHWAH, NEW JERSEY

2001

TYPE DESIGN • CASA PETTA

COVER DESIGN • CHERYL FINBOW

LIBRARY OF CONGRESS CATALOGING-IN-PUBLICATION DATA

Edwards, Tilden.
    Spiritual director, spiritual companion : guide to tending the soul / by Tilden Edwards.
        p. cm.
    Includes bibliographical references (p.).
    ISBN 0-8091-4011-X (alk. paper)
    1. Spiritual direction. I. Title.
BV5053.E37 2001
253.5'3—dc21

00-051476

Published by Paulist Press
997 Macarthur Boulevard
Mahwah, New Jersey 07430

www.paulistpress.com

Printed and bound in the
United States of America

CONTENTS

This book is written with special gratitude for the inspiration of the many beautiful souls in the Shalem Institute's Spiritual Guidance Program since its beginning in 1978.

INTRODUCTION

The small group prayed and meditated together every week. At the end of each two-hour gathering the members had a little time to share some of their experience and questions. This was very valuable to all the laypeople, clergy, and religious community members in that ecumenical gathering. But there were twenty people, and they didn't have enough time or sense of mutual accountability to go into one another's spiritual lives in an ongoing way. Many members sensed that they needed to be with someone alone (or at least with far fewer people) with whom they could regularly probe the Spirit's movements in their lives. Each of these people found a spiritual companion to complement the group's life. In time some found others coming to them with their spiritual lives, and they often felt called to be spiritual companions for them. For many a sense of inadequacy accompanied this sense of call to what seemed like an awesome responsibility for attending another person's life in God. They felt the need for deeper grounding in the Spirit's presence as they listened to others, for more learning about the ministry of spiritual companionship, and for sharing their experience with other companions. Out of this need peer groups for spiritual directors were formed to help one another. Eventually a major program came into being to assist the formation of directors.

That first group met in 1973. It was the embryonic beginning of what later became the Shalem Institute for Spiritual Formation. The first program for spiritual directors, called the Spiritual Guidance Program, began its first class in 1978, at a time when there were almost no models for such a program, especially with our emphasis on contemplative grounding. That two-year program has continued ever since. Those of us privileged to lead it have had the opportunity to probe this ancient-yet-new ministry and discipline of spiritual companionship from many vantage points. Three of us have written books on the subject: *Care of Mind, Care of Spirit* by Gerald May, *Group Spiritual Direction* by Rose Mary Dougherty, and my own *Spiritual Friend*.

Spiritual Friend was published in 1980, at the beginning of the first Spiritual Guidance Program. In this new book I am attempting to provide a fresh basic text for spiritual directors and directees that views spiritual direction and its context of the spiritual life and modern culture from the vantage point of twenty additional years of experience. It is not meant to be a definitive work. It is meant to complement other fine writings. I have included a selected bibliography of many of these other books in appendix C.

The most distinctive contributions of this book will focus on the nature of soul, on the ways we know a spiritual experience, on the different layers of community experience that a person brings to spiritual direction, and on an overall contemplative stance. Beyond these themes I will describe a range of ways to nurture the soul, offer many practical suggestions concerning the way we are present with a directee, and provide some ways of recognizing an authentic spiritual companion. You will also find a brief history of this special ministry and a view of its future. Finally, I have included in the appendices some further resources for spiritual directors, a structure for spiritual director/peer group meetings, and, as mentioned, a selective bibliography.

Each chapter has enough coherence to be understood on its own and can be read separately from the others, depending upon your interests. At the same time, the chapters are tied together by a common grounding in a contemplative orientation, for which I will try to provide an understanding in chapter one. Chapters two and three, "Who Are We?" and "How Do We Know?", are the most theoretical chapters, wherein I try to provide a basic understanding of our soul-ful nature and the different ways our minds and hearts touch a spiritual experience. Spiritual companionship usually will not be dealt with directly in these two chapters, except in the latter part of chapter three in the discussion of the process of discernment. Much of the spiritual theology reflected in these two chapters has emerged from my own reflection in recent years, grounded in an historic contemplative orientation.

I will be using the various names for this spiritual relationship interchangeably, such as spiritual companions, spiritual directors (and directees), spiritual guides, spiritual friends, and soul friends. The tradition of the early desert fathers and mothers and of some Eastern Orthodox churches would add the titles of spiritual fathers and mothers. In some Evangelical Protestant churches the relationship at least obliquely connects with what is called "shepherding" or "discipling." We need to feel free to use whatever descriptive name seems most understandable among those with whom we are likely to use it, as long as *we* are clear about the intent of what it is we are offering in this relationship.

I will be speaking of spiritual companionship within an ecumenical Christian framework. However, in the "Communal Circles" chapter (chapter seven) I have included a section on spiritual companionship in other major religious traditions and the relation of these traditions to a Christian framework. There is a new interest in this practice in some parts of the Jewish community today, and Jews and other non-Christians hopefully will find some worthwhile content for themselves in this book that can be translated into their own situations. There are also a number of people conditioned in a different major faith tradition who for various reasons seek companionship across faith lines. Another phenomenon is a growing number of Christians who have been exposed to the perspectives and practices of other faiths and bring this experience to spiritual direction.

Amidst the growing need for soul friends and in face of the explosive numbers of new programs appearing to further this ministry, I believe it is important to present spiritual direction as the profound and subtle charism it has been in the best of Christian spiritual tradition. In supporting the deepening process of directors, I think we need to avoid the temptation of diminishing the inherent mystery and freedom of our relation with the divine through trying to overunderstand or control this relationship or the spiritual life. I believe that the director's passionate givenness to God in trust, together with a sense of call to spiritual companionship, are much more crucial for an authentic spiritual direction relationship than any particular learned knowledge and skills. Having said this, I would also hold up the knowledge and skills symbolized by the contents of this book as potentially needed and valuable assets for a spiritual director. I think, though, they need to surround and never displace a core open availability for the One whom we can honor but never domesticate.

I am deeply indebted to the many gifted staff and participants of Shalem's Spiritual Guidance Program for all I have learned from them over the years and to Gerald May, Rose Mary Dougherty, and my wife, Mary, for their many insights in reviewing the manuscript.

Tilden Edwards
Shalem Institute for Spiritual Formation
Bethesda, Maryland

CHAPTER 1

WHAT IS SPIRITUAL COMPANIONSHIP, AND HOW HAS IT EVOLVED?

The Nature of Soul Friendship and Its Theological Ground •

Perhaps the greatest paradox of human life is the discovery that what is most substantial about us is most elusive. I am speaking of our deep souls: that essence of our being that transcends but is integrally part of all our visible dimensions of body, will, mind, and feelings. The deep human soul is like the essence of the holy mountain where Moses was commanded to take off his shoes. It is too sacred and intimate for our consciousness to truly grasp. We find it shrouded in cloud and fire that leaves our senses disoriented and our hearts vulnerable. Yet in the midst of this loss of our controls and definitions we find our intrinsic connection with creation and the Gracious One who gives and pervades it. Then even our controls and definitions are seen to be ultimately indivisible from the pervasive divine Presence.

Appreciation of this soul-reality (which I will speak more about in the next chapter) comes as a gift. Being part of a spiritual community of people who appreciate the soul helps us embrace and live more fully out of its reality. Living out of soul-depth is not easy. Much in our psyches and cultures tempts or confuses us into taking our cues for living from shallower ground. Even when we want to live from the Holy Spirit's movements in our souls, this inner guidance is often obscure, confusing, or completely nonapparent to our consciousness. Also, the outer guidance found in the writings of saints and theologians is often unclear as to how it might apply to us at a particular time. So we yearn for a soul-friend with whom we can share our desire for the Holy One and with whom we can try to identify and embrace the hints of divine Presence and invitation in our lives. Neither soul-friends nor anyone else can fully enter our deep soul space. However, they can listen to our articulations of it, silently open these to God as soon as they are heard, and occasionally speak when something is heard in that openness that seems to be meant for the directee.

The ministry of spiritual direction can be understood as the meeting of two or more people whose desire is to prayerfully listen for the movements of the Holy Spirit in all areas of a person's life (not just in their formal prayer life). It is a three-way relationship: among the *true* director who is the Holy Spirit (which in Christian tradition is the Spirit of Christ present in and among us), and the human director (who listens for the *directions* of the Spirit with the directee), and the directee. The interpretive framework of this relationship is seeded by understandings of the spiritual life found in scripture and in the lives and writings of great saints and theologians. The director is a companion along the pilgrim's way, wanting to be directly open along with the directee to the Spirit-undercurrents flowing through the happenings of the directee's life.

These currents provide glimpses of divine love and beauty, of particular callings to fuller communion and compassion, and glimpses of the illusions and willfulness that we are being invited to relinquish as this is empowered—those things that impede our soul-fullness. As these currents are explored together, the directees' responses to what is being shown can be noticed: what they are wanting and fearing, suffering and hoping, waiting for and acting upon. Such attention together requires a fundamental trust on the part of both director and directee that God is, that God is for us, and that God's Spirit is actively at work in our lives, within the context of our God-given freedom.

In our freedom and God's obscurity we can confusedly or willfully choose a way that narrows our consciousness and responsiveness to the divine. We might find ourselves encountering forces so willfully separated in intent from God that we call them evil and see the need to resist them. But neither the reality of our off-target, little-ego selves nor of any kind of evil force need remove us from a fundamental trust that we are an overflow, a unique form, of divine love, the love that for Christians is seen as incarnate for humanity with special power in Jesus Christ.

Any force, in the mysterious freedom of creation, that refuses an embracing of this radiant love, nonetheless is connected with that love, because I believe that love finally is all there is. God is one. God is love. Divine love creates only love. Part of love is the freedom rather than the compulsion to embrace love. We see the extreme free rejection of that love in the one who is personified as Satan. In that rejection he is left in the hell of absorption in his own self-centered power and in using it to tempt others to separate from the great Love and from authentic loving community.

But even the redemption of Satan is prayed for in Eastern Orthodox tradition. He and all evil powers are still in a hidden relationship with the great Love that created them, the Love that reverences our freedom as essential to its nature, regardless of the consequences.[1]

We cannot fathom all that God means by love, and so we struggle hard to see it in what we do not like, or at least to trust it as the divine foundation of all we see, beyond its warping by human willfulness and illusion. Our scripturally nourished trust is that in the end, love will be fully manifest; it will be all in all. Trust in such love is the living ground of spiritual direction.

Contemplative Orientation •

A contemplative understanding is seen in this book as a particularly valuable orientation for the deeper spiritual life. In the broadest spiritual sense, a contemplative orientation refers to a direct, immediate, intentional relationship with the divine Mystery at the heart of reality. It involves a givenness to God in the moment, a "continually renewed immediacy" as Thomas Kelly put it in his *Testament of Devotion*. It is a simple, open presence to what is, a presence that can accommodate all that is, a presence that is dedicated to the ultimate loving Source that pervades what is.

When this immediate open presence exists, it sometimes leads us to receive intimations of the larger Presence through our senses, feelings, images, memories, and movements of will in the moment. Our relationship with the larger Presence, God, is just as alive and intimate in the *formless,* seemingly empty spaces *between* our perceptions, images, and actions. This Presence is deeper and fuller than any of our interpretations of it. In contemplative presence we rest in a naked trust of God's loving mystery in the moment, before, within, and beyond any of our images of it. Through all that happens we seek to abide in the larger spacious Presence, which is so substantially and intimately woven through our experience, yet so beyond our grasp. In a more specifically Christian context, we can speak of our immediate involvement with the Holy Spirit, who is God's radiant presence for us, incarnate in Christ and mysteriously manifest in ourselves and in all of creation.

We see this contemplative dimension in Hebrew and Christian scripture and tradition whenever people are trying to describe personal and group encounters that are ultimately beyond their comprehension, and yet which they experience as utterly real and communicative in the moment. They touch and trust a transcendent, loving reality at work, inviting them into intimate communion and active loving and appreciation of life. As I have inferred, such encounters are not necessarily experienced by our imagination or senses. They may be found in what seem like emptiness and darkness. They also may be found in our yearning for this beyondness-in-our-midst, which is trusted as a desire planted in us by the divine Beloved.

Given what I have said about contemplation, we can see that it has at least two different connotations. The first is as a way of being present in the moment; the second is the experience of God's initiatives in the moment, which has been called "infused" contemplation. It is in the former sense, that is, as an orientation to the Real One in the immediate moment, whether anything is consciously gifted experientially or not in that time, that I will normally be referring when I speak of contemplation.

Further perspectives on contemplative understanding of the spiritual life will be spread throughout this book in relation to different aspects of the spiritual direction relationship and our evolving experience.

Historical Roots •

In the broadest sense I'm sure that human beings have always sought out one another to ponder the mysteries of their soul-experience. As we will see later in this book, it has been a practice in one form or another in every deep spiritual tradition. Informally and as an often unnamed occasional practice, the ministry of spiritual direction I believe has been present in every Christian tradition.

Hebrew Scripture

"You guide me with your counsel..." (Ps 73:24).

"Your decrees are my delight, they are my counselors" (Ps 119:24).

"Give your servant therefore an understanding [listening, discerning] heart/mind" (1 Kgs 3:9).

These verses perhaps summarize the abiding sense of guidance in Hebraic tradition: the direct guidance from God and from his revealed Torah (the first five books of the Bible), lived out in a covenanted community. The role of spiritual/moral counselor (whether as priest, prophet, wisdom figure, or rabbi) involves expected obedience, not to the guide bearing individual authority, but to his reasoned teachings and interpretations of the Law or to his ecstatic, prophetic calls back to it.[2]

Later guidance given by Wisdom literature (Proverbs, Job, Ecclesiastes, etc.) should be mentioned separately, since its focus on reverent attitudes and moral habits does not necessarily draw from the Torah but is a parallel stream of wisdom drawn from a large Near Eastern pool. See, for example, Ecclesiasticus 6:5–17 on friendship, which includes this gem: "Let your acquaintances be many, but your advisers one in a thousand."

A more directly mystical source of divine guidance is found in Moses' request for the Torah Giver's name

(Exod 3:14). The answer was a finally untranslatable sound, which the tradition has carried as "I am who I am," or "The One who causes to be." The open-endedness of this revealed name in effect protects the divine Mystery from human projection. Yet the revealed, personal Mystery has substance, guiding in cloud by day and fire by night. This ultimately unnamable (in the sense of a name that can capture the eternal essence of divine reality) yet trustworthy One, surrounding us by benevolent guidelines for a way of life in human/divine covenant, has remained the core of Jewish and the framework for Christian spirituality. It gradually replaced guidance by magic, oracle, and lots.

The Law itself was seen in more mystical terms periodically at least from the time of Philo, the influential first-century Alexandrian Jewish exegete. For him, the moral purification afforded by living in the Law is done by God, as a way of making room for his transcendent Spirit to live in us.[3]

Jesus as Guide

Jesus assumed the framework of Torah and covenant community, interpreting them in the light of his sense of the growing reign of God. That reign, as he conveyed it, involved a great human/divine intimacy. He spoke of God with the unusually familiar "abba," "dear father," or "daddy." He saw himself in God, and himself in his disciples, and they in him. He and light were one in the transfiguration. The powers of the Holy One flowed through him in the gospel accounts: for healing, reconciliation, justice, resurrection, and recognition of true life. Jesus promised the abiding bridging of the human/divine chasm through the indwelling of God as Holy Spirit.

In these ways Jesus raised to central focus that unmediated strand of direct guidance and intimacy found in Moses and the prophets, not thereby throwing out the guidance framework of Torah, but drawing out its inner meaning and context in light of his awareness. As Moses' firsthand intimacy with the Holy One provided unmediated context for the gift to the people of mediated Law and its holy way of life, so Jesus' firsthand awareness and vocation in the Holy One provided the unmediated context for the gifts of mediated acts of redemption, interpretation of the Law, and the promise of an eternally present inner Advocate welling up in us, the Holy Spirit, in a dawning New Age.

Thus in the transfiguration Jesus was caught up in light, speaking with Moses and with the other prime exemplar of such divine intimacy in Hebrew scripture, Elijah (who heard God in a still, small murmur and is the one person in Hebrew scripture said never to have died).

And yet there is no grand self-deification. The "untranslatable name" of the Holy One is preserved at the same time as the unique divine intimacy and gifts are manifest. Jesus knows his finitude as a human being: He must suffer and die; he must struggle to communicate day by day, often unsuccessfully, with hard-hearted, fearful, and uncomprehending people, including his own followers. As seen in the Garden of Gethsemane, he must struggle with his own will and the will of God. He rebukes a man for calling him good: "No one is good but God alone" (Mark 10:18).

This then is the basic context, as I see it, for Jesus' guidance: the paradoxical transcendence and intimacy of God, and its fruits apparent in Jesus' interpretation of Hebrew scripture, in his visionary capacity for discernment of divine calling, and in his Spirit-empowered compassion brought to its fullness in the way he held all life together on the cross, in empowering forgiveness. Since we have only recorded fragments of his life, what we see is a patchwork of different situations in which he responds uniquely to each person and situation with mind- and soul-opening questions and comments and with symbolic and healing acts.

In this way he provides a pattern for Christian life: each of us needs a special "saving" word, question, or act at the right moments in our lives. What I need may be contradictory to what another needs. And yet this is not simply subjective individualism; it is within the framework of a shared covenant with a revealed yet mysterious guiding Presence. Jesus often used parables because these are concrete and open-ended compared to logically linear statements. They mediate the ineffable loving Mystery to us in different ways, as we are ready to hear, always leaving a little mystery left over.

Jesus chose and cultivated an inner circle of disciples for special guidance, preparing them to succeed him. Their recorded imperfections show us the willingness of Jesus to trust that the Spirit can show itself through fragile human vessels. After a period of formation he dared to call these disciples friends rather than servants, exhorting them to go and bear fruit that abides (John 15:15f.). This quality of acceptance can give all of us a little more confidence when we see our own limitations in the face of what seems like a call to be available for the spiritual life of others. Jesus reinforces this in his declaration that when he leaves, the Holy Spirit will infuse us and the Spirit of truth will lead us into all the truth (John 16:13). In our trust in God through this Spirit, we will do even greater works than Jesus (John 14:12).

Jesus' ministry has marked the path of spiritual guidance taken in church history. Through a great variety of forms, these have been some of the mainstream constants:

1. a sense of serving and sharing with rather than "lording it over" another, even when there has been a context of obedience to the guide;

2. confidence in the human capacity and calling to be in contact with the Holy One, and to mediate the Presence to one another through word, sacrament, and deed.

We also see a strong historical current in church history, as in Jesus himself, of an integral relation of moral and spiritual development; a vision of bearing, struggling hope in the final reconciliation of all creation to its intimate Source; and a willingness to work with all sorts and conditions of people.

Paul of Tarsus

St. Paul, who had no human contact with Jesus but a profound inner one, is our other primary New Testament source for spiritual guidance. He held a developmental view of human spiritual life. Paul speaks of the *napioi,* the beginners, who need to be fed with milk; and the *teleoi,* the mature, who can be fed solid food, those with Spirit-filled knowledge (1 Cor 2:13–16; 3:2; Eph 4:13–15; Col 1:10).

The *teleoi* have moved ever more decisively from the way of the "flesh," that is, the way of enslavement to blind, human, destructive passions, to the way of the "spirit," where these passions have been transmuted into compassion and where law is transformed into an undergirding awareness of grace, unmerited gift. The *teleoi* are hopeful for the full revelation of God, a hope that encourages patience in suffering. They are aware of being mystically "in Christ," a complementary, serving part of a corporate Body. Such are the fruits of those who have "died to sin" and "the old Adam" and "live to God" in "the new humanity."

Paul exhorted the struggling early Gentile-dominated churches, lacking the common conditioning and guidance of Jewish tradition, to provide spiritual guidance and correction for one another, an emphasis passed down through the history of spiritual guidance as "mutual edification" and "fraternal correction." However, often it seems that *not*

this guidance was restricted historically to moral admonition, cut off from the context of the gracious, intimate, liberating, guiding presence of the Spirit. The deeper life invited by the Spirit could be smothered in this separation of the moral and spiritual life.

Greek and Roman Contributions

Seeking the truth through a kind of spiritual friendship was greatly valued among ancient Greek and Roman writers. Perhaps the most important single contribution comes from Cicero's dialogue *On Friendship.* His advocacy of a deep, loyal friendship rooted in love without corrupting expedient motives was rewritten by the great twelfth-century English Cistercian Abbot, Aelred of Rievaulx and called *On Spiritual Friendship,* which holds closely to the form and much of the substance of its Roman inspirer.

Kant's value of intent?

Aelred believed that the love of friendship springs directly from God, coming closer to the love of the saints in heaven than most other loves. True friendship combines charity and good will, and is possible only between those who resist the sin and greed that would destroy it. It is "mutual harmony in affairs human and divine coupled with benevolence and charity." Spiritual friendship is distinguished from carnal friendship that springs from mutual harmony in vice, and from worldly friendship that is enkindled by the hope of gain.

typology of love

virtues

Four qualities must be tested in a friend: loyalty, right intention, discretion, and patience. Aelred brilliantly elaborates each of these. He quotes St. Ambrose's insight that friendships among the poor are generally more secure than those among the rich, since poverty takes away the hope of gain in such a way as not to decrease the love of friendship but rather to increase it. Ambrose also is quoted favorably in terms of correcting vice in a friend: "The wounds inflicted by a friend are more tolerable than the kisses of flatterers. Therefore correct the erring friend."[4]

Such intimate spiritual friendship in monastic settings rarely was advocated, given the alleged dangers of factionalism, favoritism, and sexual expression. Experience with false, distorted friendship led monastic norms to stress an exclusive desire for God at the expense of loving friendship. But friendship had a certain flowering in the eleventh and twelfth centuries, especially through Anselm of Canterbury, Bernard of Clairvaux, and William of St. Thierry, along with Aelred. By the late Middle Ages and the Counter-Reformation, however, friendships of any sort were banned from the cloister and the most ordinary of personal contacts were viewed with deep suspicion.[5]

This depersonalization was bolstered by an impersonal, abstract theology and moral legalism that was dominant with Roman Catholics from the sixteenth-century Council of Trent right up to the Second Vatican Council. I think such depersonalization was dominant in different ways in many Protestant traditions as well. Spiritual companionship in this context often involved a distancing that was a far cry from Aelred's friendship. There were many important exceptions to this trend, however, as seen, for example, in some of the great historic spiritual friendships between holy men and women, such as John of the Cross and Teresa of Avila, St. Jane de Chantal and Francis de Sales, and in the letters and other writings of more intimate relationships that we find from this period, including those from the great sixteenth-and seventeenth-century Roman Catholic schools of spirituality. A more personal sense of human and divine relationship can also be inferred among Protestant Pietists, Quakers, in segments of the Anglican and other Protestant pastoral traditions, and in the Eastern Orthodox continuation of the early desert tradition of the spiritual father and mother. This desert tradition needs special attention in this history of spiritual friendship.

The Desert Seeds

As a formal, disciplined, named, regular practice, spiritual direction (as opposed to individual confession) appears to have been rare outside of ordained ministry and vowed religious communities until the twentieth century. Its historical origin as an intentional Christian practice is found with what were mostly laypeople who created the radical tradition of desert spirituality.

ironic

Beginning in the third century and growing until the Moslem conquest, thousands of Christians left the towns of the Roman Empire and other nearby Christian lands to seek the depths of their souls in God, living alone in desert caves or in loose, small communities in North Africa and the Near East. This tide grew especially after the church became established in the empire and lost much of its uncompromised fervor.

Scripture at times encourages the purgative, illuminative value of such living beyond the force of prevailing social structure, as we see in the life and teachings of John the Baptist, Jesus, and Paul, and in certain prophets before them. We also see this cleansing of sight and will in the desert of Exodus times, when the Hebrew people, after escaping from the oppressive Egyptian social structure, wandered in the wilderness, where they were tested and given significant revelations.

Jesus encouraged surrender of the attached worldly self and its ambition, status, complacency, and material wealth, replacing these with a seeking of the kingdom of God. Paul exhorted the Thessalonians to pray without ceasing (1 Thess 5:17), which the desert fathers and mothers tried to do, through early versions of the Jesus Prayer and other practices.

In the sparseness of Near Eastern and North African desert areas, these radical God-seekers usually lived a life of solitude, prayer, scriptural recitation, simple manual work, and humble simplicity. Behind these practices was a sense of firsthand spiritual combat, martyrdom of the false self, and radical freedom for God.

This new intensity had no community womb and lineage of living spiritual masters to guide it in its inception. The abbas (fathers) and ammas (mothers) of the desert had to be courageous, charismatic pioneers of the Spirit, in effect, breaking ground for those who would follow. Though St. Antony of Egypt in the fourth century was not the first of these, he was one of the early pioneers, and the one we know most about.[6] After he had spent many years in solitude, other desert seekers pleaded with him to come out from his walled-in cell in an abandoned fort and guide them, which he did.

> When he emerged from the fort, his soul was pure: neither contracted by grief, dissipated by pleasure, nor pervaded by jollity or dejection. He was completely under control, guided by reason.... He performed healings, exorcism, comforting, reconciling.... To all he was a father and guide.[7]

There we see the birth of the desert abba and the search for him by those needing help in the arduous, dangerous, promising, tempting life of desert spiritual combat. Some, like Antony, became so transparent to God that others sought them out for advice or begged to become their spiritual children and live close by, under their direction. The close relationships that developed could include regular sharing of the disciple's thoughts and feelings in great detail and the willingness to trust the guide's intuitions about what the disciple needed to understand and do in order to deepen their life in God.[8]

Though the abba's weight on obedience by the disciple is beyond what most democratically conditioned people would easily accept today, there can be value in voluntary, temporary submission to a trusted, highly experienced guide beyond the dangers of such submission. This practice is corroborated in Eastern as well as Western spiritual experience. The true abba seemed to provide a kind of ego shock treatment to help the disciple eventually mutate from his false, illusory self, from belief in a pretentious, idolatrous, protected self-image, toward a larger, freer and "humbly confident" trust and realization of his being in God.

This involved not just advice, but insistence that the disciple learn for himself, by staying in the "fiery furnace and pillar of cloud" of his cell (Antony), and in fasting and prayer, facing through to the raw truth firsthand. Obedience and trust with a caring, experienced abba could help you "face through" all the way.[9]

Echoes of the Desert Tradition

The tradition of the desert spiritual father and mother as solitary charismatic persons living on the margins of society has continued to exist spottily throughout the church's history. In more recent times one place we have seen them is in the Russian *poustinikki*, especially in the nineteenth and early twentieth centuries. These people were drawn from all walks of life to poverty and solitude on behalf of others. They normally would move to a hut, a *poustinia* (a desert place) away from the town. Here he or she would live in solitude, but not in isolation. The Russian word for solitude means "being with everybody."

The *poustinik* lived in solitude, but with the people in intercessory prayer, counsel, and service. By tradition the latch was always off the door; the *poustinik's* priority at any time was his neighbor's need. At times the *poustinik* would be expected to come out with a public "word from the Lord" for the community.

Perhaps the closest Western church parallel was the medieval English anchorite or anchoress (Julian of Norwich being the most famous), often attached to village churches, living in contemplative solitude for life, yet often available for counsel. One current adaptation of that tradition is found in the Madonna House community based in Ontario, Canada, founded by Catherine de Hueck Doherty, whose heritage was both Russian Orthodox and Roman Catholic.[10]

The desert father and mother also evolved into the monastic tradition's abbot and abbess, drawing into themselves both the discernment function of the desert father/mother and the organizational authority of a ruler. The desert inheritance probably is most apparent today in Eastern Orthodox, Coptic, and Ethiopian monastic traditions.

The gathered community as a source of spiritual guidance, seen throughout scripture and tradition, is brought to particular intensity in monasticism. The intensity of the pre-Constantinian church's mutual edification and the desert father/mother's personal mentoring was succeeded by monastic communities of mostly laypeople, guided by a "Rule" of life. This life was viewed not so much as a new way, but in fact as continuous with the old way of the apostles, persevering together in prayer, community of goods, and breaking of bread (Acts 2:42).[11]

The practice of one-to-one guidance within the community's life was known from the earliest days. A right to and responsibility for the practice often was written into the monastic Rules themselves. It complemented various forms of group guidance. In the pre-Constantinian churches and in later Protestant communities, this one-to-one guidance apparently was more of an informal, occasional meeting on a needs basis. In the desert and in monastic communities this counsel often took on a more serious and sometimes more regular character—an opportunity to pour out one's soul in confession and in description of inner motivations—aimed at recognizing and relieving obstacles to progress toward holiness.

Something of this regularized intent is found later in the early left wing of the Reformation and in the eighteenth-century Methodist small-group meetings for mutual edification and correction (and their various Protestant successors).

The context of this sustained personal guidance was an integral system of moral and spiritual assumptions, to which both director and directee were committed as a basis for living "into" spiritual truth. Their work together was but one part of a reinforcing way of life that was providing guidance all the time. The up-front focus was the person's gradual transfiguration into communion with God in Christ, and its overflow into spontaneous and vocational charity. Every dimension of a person's life was touched, to the degree that the desert tradition was followed, so that nothing would be withheld from the director's sight or, by implication, from one's own sight.

Confession was often included (a function later usually separated from that of spiritual direction). The dual aim of confession, when authentic, was acceptance of accountability for one's own life and a desire to let go of whatever had come between one and the loving reality of God, neighbor, and true self. Its hoped-for result was forgiveness, recovery, healing, purification, peace, and a capacity for freshly innocent presence.

This relationship with the monastic director and confessor has certain parallels with the openness of a modern therapeutic relationship. The literature also indicates an awareness of both unconscious and conscious motives long before Freud. Cassian, for example, as early as the fifth century,

looked to dream imagery and desires for evidence of unconscious maladies of the soul. But the aim was not only their
relief, but their replacement by virtuous attitudes and deeds.
Monastic spiritual guidance differs from modern therapy in
its integral context of values and community life and, within
this context, in the director's knowledge of the person
through great daily intimacy, often over many years. Such a
context provides opportunities for dealing holistically with
the person and at its best allows for the ever more subtle
process of deep oral transmission of the heart of the Gospel,
to the degree that it is embodied in the director.

The spiritual guide could approach this transmission
with great versatility. Basil illustrates this when he says,
"Know that humility, authority, rebuke, exhortation, compassion, freedom of speech, kindness, severity, in a word
everything has its own time."[12]

In unenlightened hands this guidance process could
turn into moralism, legalism, and tyranny of soul, with
inadequate diagnosis and prescription. In the hands of a
true master, this process could provide for the liberation
and preparation of great human hearts. Thomas Merton
says in this regard, "The director, if not essential for the
spiritual life, is considered in practice to have had a deci-
sive part to play in the lives of saints and mystics, with a
few notable exceptions. [Great directors] have clearly exer-
cised a providential function in the lives not only of individuals but also of religious congregations and of certain
social milieux, indeed of the church itself."[13]

The Rise of Spiritual Direction in Our Time •

In a period of accelerated and continual change such as
the one in which we are now living, I believe there is an
instinctual urge to search for the wheat as the chaff is

blown away in the winds of change or, to shift the image a bit, to find deeper roots that will not be torn up by the winds and leave us adrift. Within the various churches, one way that this instinct has been lived out has been to become Fundamentalist: holding onto a particular absolutist and narrow theological view of reality and behavior and denying the Holy Spirit's positive presence amidst the cataclysmic shifts underway. At the other end of the church spectrum people's response has been to question and reconstellate what is real and believable in the light of their expanding cultural horizons, trusting that the Holy Spirit is at work in the current situation and that this work needs to be discerned and embraced.

A dedicated layperson who I think would see herself at this second end of the spectrum recently told me that she stands within her church, but her horizon is much larger. Her sensing of the Spirit's presence in many of the changes she sees has left her open not only to the Spirit's presence in the church, but more open to its presence in the world beyond the church. She listens for that presence in non-Christian deep spiritual traditions, in nature, in various human movements that arise, and in her own experience.

This woman, I think, is a growing kind of new Christian who values the particularity of her own tradition as a vital orienting platform in life, yet who feels that she is part of the globalization of life today, wherein we have the full richness of the human spiritual heritage to call upon and the vitality of the Spirit at work in the world wherever loving light shows itself. Her grounding as a Christian gives her a way to claim a discerning way of life through all the possibilities, a life in which Christ is embraced as her "main man" (or "main person"), if I can put it that way: the One to whose Spirit she turns for empowerment of wise loving and trusting that it is God's Spirit, the One to whom she is vulnerable and committed. But the nature of Christ has grown larger for her, larger than the church has often shown her. And her understanding of the largeness of her own soul has grown also.

An older Roman Catholic sister from another country recently told me that, for her, only the sky is large enough to be an icon of God. The universe has been shown to be so vast, the spectrum of human experience so great, that no doctrine feels adequate to carry the fullness of spiritual truth at this point in her life.

These two people both desire to go deeper and become freer in the life of their souls with God. They are prime candidates for spiritual companionship today, along with thousands of others from all parts of the theological spectrum who don't have such a bold vision, yet who sense that they are unique children of God with an ongoing human journey under the Spirit's guidance. They want to understand and embrace their spiritual journey as best they can. In appreciating their uniqueness and the mystery of the Spirit's ways with them, they realize they are always standing on a frontier.

For many non-Fundamentalist religious seekers, just as for scientists today, there is a greater sense of mystery than of confident clarity about the deep truths of life than there was a few decades ago. At the same time there is often a sense that at the heart of that mystery there is One who is trustworthy, ever drawing us into life-giving ways.

Two people gathered together for directly attending the Spirit at work in one or both of their lives is the church in its smallest communal form ("Where two or three are gathered together in my name, I am there among them" Matt 18:20). In a time of great ferment, we could say that this minimal gathering is an opportunity to find the wheat amidst the chaff in the chaos of life, a chance to sink our roots deeper in heaven, where "moth and rust don't consume" (Matt 6:19). It's a sort of "back to basics" movement, where people gather in the simplest form and look at their own firsthand experience for signs of the true wind of the Spirit, the wind that both purifies and plants seeds that are meant to grow into trees whose roots reach to the living waters.

Contributors to the Growth of Spiritual Direction

Beyond this more foundational root for the explosive increase in the ministry and discipline of spiritual direction in recent decades, there are a number of specific contributors to its growth today, especially among the laity. These contributors include:

1. Popular spiritual and religious educational movements that lead people to want ongoing help with their spiritual lives, such as Cursillo, the charismatic movement, Alcoholics Anonymous and similar organizations, and various spiritual formation programs.

2. A stronger theological sense of lay life and ministry as an ever deepening spiritual endeavor, reflecting a universal call to holiness.

3. A greater awareness and openness to spiritual practices across denominational and interfaith lines. For example, a great many Protestant churches have become supportive of spiritual direction as a ministry and practice, even though historically this has not been a formal, regular practice in most of them.

4. A growing need for help in making spiritually authentic choices amidst the myriad cultural and psychic pressures and shifting, pluralistic values of contemporary life, including different values within the church itself.

5. The influence of psychological counseling, with its sense of the human journey as one of ongoing change,

growth, and self-reflection, and a sense of the goodness of having someone to help you look at your life. If this is true for one's emotional life, then why not for one's spiritual life as well?

6. The rise of women to positions of spiritual leadership and to much spiritual exploration in the modern world. Combining this reality with the valuation of personal intimacy with God and people that seems to be more prevalent in many women's lives than in men's, we see how the ministry and practice of spiritual direction becomes a natural arena for spiritual reflection among women. The great growth in this ministry, both as directors and as directees, I believe has been much more apparent among women than men.

7. The presence of respected spiritual directors in the last few decades, primarily members of religious communities in the early years (both men and women) but now including many more laypeople, chaplains, and pastors, with a sense of calling to support the increase of this ministry, including the support of gifted laypeople as spiritual directors, through writings about spiritual direction as well as through the organization of training programs for spiritual directors.

For such reasons as these spiritual direction has become a vital dimension of the maturing spiritual life for many thousands of people today. I don't believe it is a passing fad. It has endured in one form or another since the early days of the church, and its value is corroborated by every other deep spiritual tradition. Once experienced in an authentic form, I think its value will become apparent to most people.

Even for those who avail themselves of spiritual direction only at special points of need in their lives, it can still be appreciated as one of the vital disciplines of the church. It is not needed by everyone as a formal practice, but it is important that it be visible and available for those who are in need of spiritual companionship. Its cumulative, long-term fruits for the well-being and deepening of church, family, and societal life are incalculable. It supports, tests, and encourages our direct relationship with God and the truth of our own souls. It helps us to risk embracing the often disorienting transformations that emerge from becoming vulnerable to the most subtle yet substantial reality of our lives: our soul-life in God.

Differences from Psychological Counseling •

Modern psychological counseling, in its many forms, has had a great impact on the way we see and reflect on ourselves and others. The origins of modern psychological study and counseling often in effect assume the autonomy of human beings from spiritual forces. Human reality is understood in terms of physiological, intrapsychic and interhuman forces. The mainstream of psychological history focuses on understanding personal and social dysfunctionality and how this might be resolved through various kinds of therapeutic intervention.

There is no shared vision of human fullness in this movement. The focus on disease often has been seen in relation to implicit cultural standards of health and well-being. In recent decades there has been a growing strand of concern among counselors for a vision of human wholeness and healing that moves beyond the focus of discrete psychological problems and their resolution. This trend has also taken more seriously the potential validity of a relationship to transcendent Spirit as part of human reality, healing, and fullness. As a result the gap that once was more obviously present between counseling and spiritual assumptions about human nature I believe has been diminishing.

This closeness sometimes involves confusion, however, as when spiritual resources are approached exclusively in a utilitarian way as instruments of the small self's predetermined ends, as if this were the central purpose of relationship with the divine. This contrasts with the centrality of identification with and givenness to divine love, wherever it may lead, that is so central in classical spiritual direction. In the latter view the little-ego self is a vessel of a deeper self in God, not vice-versa.

Perhaps the clearest distinction that continues to exist between different kinds of counseling and spiritual direction is one of focus and function. Counseling is focused primarily on our emotional hang-ups—the ways we are limited in our capacity to cope with our inner psychological forces and with other people. We go to a counselor (psychologist, psychiatrist, clinical social worker, pastoral counselor, etc.) to try and gain insight and greater flexibility related to the way we function in daily living. A divine force may be accepted in the relationship, but the primary intent of paying attention to that force is to use it to help us improve our personal effectiveness.

In spiritual direction the focus is on that divine force, on God, as the integral core of our being and purpose. We go to a spiritual director because we want to become more attuned to God's Spirit in our spirit and freely live out of divine love, with the background help of scriptural interpretation and experiential spiritual tradition about what such love looks like. Spiritual direction is about healing our relationship with God, our overseparation from God, with a sense of all other kinds of human healing (and bearing of nonhealing) being related to that central healing. Its focus is not on an insular individual or social sense of wholeness, where individual or collective identity at the functional ego level is seen as the center of human reality.

Its focus is on a sense of identity that is "hidden with God in Christ," a sense of self that includes but is not ultimately defined by that ego level.

At their best, spiritual direction and various kinds of psychological counseling complement one another, and both can be seen to contribute to human well-being. Some knowledge of psychological dynamics can be helpful to both directors and directees, though this knowledge will be relative to an awareness of the surprising freedom and ways of the Holy Spirit in us. At their worst counseling and direction make contradictory or inadequate assumptions about what a fully human being is and needs. In either case, they have distinctively different histories and purposes, even as they often find themselves closer to each other today in understanding human nature than in the past.[14]

One recent psychologically oriented influence on religious people has been the categorizing of people into types based on qualities of personality and temperament. Two popular forms of type classification have been the Meyers-Briggs Type Inventory (MBTI), loosely based on Carl Jung's personality theories, which attempts to measure *preferences,* and the Enneagram, a system that claims ancient Asian spiritual sources, which, to oversimplify this sophisticated typology, could be said to describe different qualities of *energy* in us.

These resources potentially can be of value in spiritual direction to the extent that they can help people to accept their personal differences from others without feeling that there is something wrong about their own or others' differences. The Enneagram further offers challenges to spiritual growth.[15] But, as Gerald May has pointed out, they can become idols when they cease to be *descriptive* and start to become *predictive* or *prescriptive.* The attempt to tell people what kinds of prayer are right for them or ways of soul-growth that people of different Enneagram types "should" follow has the danger of trying to secure our identities in a manner that loses the hard-to-bear mysterious evolution of the ways of uncontrollable grace at the core of our lives. As with attempts to describe stages of faith development, these categorizations can be valuable to us if held lightly and not allowed to overdefine us. We are all so much more in God's eyes than any of our mental categories can encompass.

CHAPTER 2

WHO ARE WE?
THE NATURE OF SOUL

"Who are we?" or, more specifically for the purposes of this book, "Who are we *in God?*" This is the enduring, foundational human question, one that always defies our little answers. Our spiritual journeys are marked by outgrown answers and an ever new asking of the question. There is something very securing about being able to ultimately define who we are, and yet I think we are finally indefinable at our core. We are more than our minds can grasp. We are as big a mystery as God, if we are truly grown in the image of God. However disappointing this is to our security-seeking psyches, it is finally a great gift. St. Paul says that God has in mind for us more than we can possibly imagine (Eph 3:20), so we shouldn't see reality confined to what our minds can imagine and define. Then perhaps we are more available for the ongoing surprises and expansiveness that life is in God.

With this warning about any attempt to try and ultimately wrap up our identities in the tight shrouds of some definition that will always burst in the face of the full mystery of our being, I am going to offer a way of looking at who we are from the standpoint of soul. Our minds are gifts from God, and they perpetually seek to understand, so there is a gift in definitions as there is a gift in accepting the limitations of definitions. They help us to grasp at least the hem of the divine garment out of which we are made. And they help us to communicate with one another about this shared mystery.

In the past few years I have found myself using the word *soul* more and more to talk about the core of our nature. It is interesting to note how many others have been using that word more frequently in the last few years as well, not only in the religious but even more so in so-called secular circles. In the corporate world, for example, innumerable books in the past few years have taken up this word, both in terms of individual soul and of corporate soul, as central to the true life of organizations.

Why are people using and responding to this word so much today? I think behind this trend is a growing sense in the culture that there is something larger in our nature than has often been appreciated. We are much more than the definitions to which we have often been reduced by much of modern physical and behavioral science, economics, and even in practice by the church. *Soul* is the word being used to carry a sense of our larger transcendent being.

I think a word like *soul* also is needed to help bridge the gap between the divine and the human. In contemplative tradition and in the recorded firsthand experiences of the divine in human history in general we see an incredible intimacy between the divine and the human, reflected in the beginning of Hebrew Scripture in the Genesis passage where we are declared to be made in the image of God (Gen 1:27). The historical danger of reducing God to ourselves, together with an experienced sense of the otherness of God, I believe, has led to a greater emphasis on God's transcendence than on divine immanence in much of Western religious tradition. I think this transcendence is vital in reminding us that the reality of God is infinitely more than a projection of our own needs and images, infinitely more than ourselves, and beyond creation itself.

And yet God's Spirit creates us, dwells in us, shapes us, reverberates the divine image in us, draws us toward fullness in God. In this sense God is infinitely immanent, infinitely close, closer than anything we can imagine. The divine "otherness" in this intimate sense, I believe, is not found in any *real* divine distance from us. Rather, it is found in the distance created in our own minds by our ideas of the divine, and in the distance we create by our willfulness. Paradoxically, God's *otherness* lies in this sense, in a *closeness* that is beyond our imagining. Our images of the divine can themselves distance us from the divine, because God is closer than those images can convey. As St. Augustine said, God is closer to us than we are to ourselves. The Holy One is the breath of our breath, in the seed of our thought, feeling, and will, hidden infinitely deep in us, in all creation. However, God is not confined to this "insideness" of things; God is *in* and yet not *of* creation. To return to the tradition's terms, God is both transcendent and immanent.

Given this sense of the intimacy of divine reality as well as its vastness, I think we need a bridging term like *soul* to overcome the kind of overdualism between God and us that our language sets up when we only speak of "God" and "person," as though they were realities that are ultimately, not just relatively, apart from each other. *Soul* speaks of the divine and human dwelling mysteriously together in the center of our being all the time. Our deep soul accommodates God's Spirit drawing to itself our free human spirit, our personal life force.

In communal situations, we could say that the Holy Spirit alive in each soul expands its activity to encompass the community. The community's members are drawn by God's Spirit to recognize a communal soul that accommodates their human spirits and inspires them to live together in the Spirit's creative love. Perhaps we could also say that this activity of the Spirit expands beyond particular communities to all of creation; that creation itself is an interwoven, dynamic web of life with a shared soul that accommodates God's Spirit yearning for its mysterious fullness.

The great weakness and strength of the word *soul* is its vagueness of definition. The weakness is that anyone can use the word to mean anything they want. It can become so vague and empty of specific spiritual or even psychological content that it becomes a meaningless term or a confused distortion of its great reality. It can also be interpreted in a way common to much of our Greek philosophical heritage, disconnecting soul from body and leading to disuse of the word among many scripture scholars who have been afraid that this dichotomizing connotation will lose the wholeness of the human person as biblically portrayed.[1]

The strength of its vagueness is that soul's reality can never be fully grasped by the mind. Our sense of its reality recedes from the mind into the spiritual heart, and in the heart it is more apprehended than comprehended. Giving priority to such sensed apprehension over attempted controlling comprehension, I think, is a way of reverencing the mystery of soul. This inherent difficulty of definability is reflected in Albert Schweitzer's insight, "I have never seen a good definition of soul, but I know it when I feel it."[2]

Even in scripture we find the meaning of soul to be slippery, and that isn't surprising, since soul is too large and hidden to be captured by any one definition. In Hebrew Scripture (the Old Testament) there are three terms that are frequently interchanged: *nephesh,* often translated as "soul," with the frequent connotation of a human being in his/her totality, who has a *ruach* (spirit, breath) and a *leb* (heart). *Ruach* often refers to that part of a human being that relates to God, trusts, and believes. *Leb* often refers to the soul as an operating, willing force. It can also connote conscience and character. Soul and body are seen as inseparable, both emanating from God. The Creator breathes into us, as living proof that a human being is made in the image and with the life force of the Creator.

St. Paul in the New Testament makes psychological distinctions through the use of such Greek words as *pneuma,* "wind, spirit," and *psyche,* "soul" or "consciousness." Sometimes he contrasts these with *soma,* the material element of body. But none of these nor their relationships is used in a consistent way.[3]

The English word *soul* carries many rich overtones, drawn from its scriptural influences, from Greek philosophy (which, as I mentioned, could speak of the soul as an ultimately separate reality from the body), and from other European sources. The word itself, according to Webster's dictionary, ultimately is related to *sea.* That seems very appropriate when we think of the mysterious, moving, powerful, life-giving depths of the sea. For all its fuzziness, the word *soul* strikes a deep resonance in many people, as though our hearts know what it means, even if our minds can't fully grasp it.

Thomas Merton spoke to the mystery of our deep souls when he said:

> At the center of our being is a point of nothingness which is untouched by sin and by illusion, a point of pure truth, a point or spark which belongs entirely to God, which is never at our disposal, from which God disposes of our lives, which is inaccessible to

the fantasies of our own mind or the brutalities of our own will. This little point of nothingness and of absolute poverty is the pure glory of God in us.[4]

I would add that this point of nothingness in us is where we become constantly pregnant with the Holy Spirit's energy. Julian of Norwich calls the soul "Christ's most familiar home and eternal dwelling." It is the hidden open point through which God's Spirit in Christ empowers our lives. Meister Eckhart with his usual boldness says that "The soul has a capacity large enough for God to empty his entire might, the whole ground of his being, into it. This [God] does in the act of giving birth to himself spiritually in the soul," which happens when God finds the soul empty and detached enough.[5]

The great thirteenth-century mystic Rumi in effect speaks of God and the soul with different imagery. He says that we have the energy of the sun in us, but we keep knotting it up at the base of our spine.[6] In other words, God's Spirit is the sun alive in us, wanting to radiate fullness of life in and through us, asking our willingness to let go what is being held onto that impedes this radiation.

That radiation would infuse our whole being. We could say that our soul is our whole being as it is oriented toward God. Our whole being includes our bodies, our conditioned psyches, and that transcendent core of soul that orients our bodies and psyches toward wholeness and authenticity of being in God.

The theologian and psychologist Daniel Helminiak makes a very careful case for what he calls "spirit" as an empirical, constitutive dimension of our being—spirit in the sense of an openness to and anticipation of everything there is to be known and loved, everything that is true and good.[7] We could say then that every human being has an empirically verifiable spiritual nature, a capacity for the holy, which will show itself in the process of human development. It is present and active apart from any particular faith content.

This view of our human nature connects with the classic statement of the Jesuit paleontologist Teilhard de Chardin, who said in effect that we are not human beings on a spiritual journey; rather, we are spiritual beings on a human journey. He is saying, I believe, that we are spiritual (or we could say soul) beings intrinsically; this is not an imposed "add-on" to our lives. We are embodied spirits, embodied souls, on a mysterious journey from, in, and to the Holy One. Divine energy soaks us to the core, however hidden this is to our minds.

This hiddenness raises the question of why we miss this spiritual truth and call of our being so easily. This is a mystery that has no clear answer. Christian tradition speaks of the Fall, which I would see centrally as our fall from awareness of and responsiveness to God's Spirit in our souls and in creation. Modern psychology sometimes speaks of the psychic drive to homeostasis, which can be seen as in conflict with the soul's drawnness to the dynamic Allness and love of God; this drawnness can lead our psyches away from a harmonious balance of psychic forces.

We also see the psychic scars and defenses in us, sometimes externally solidified into unjust and oppressive social systems, that are in need of healing and freedom. These limitations too could affect our openness to larger spiritual reality, though I don't think they are always barriers. The Spirit can show itself through any condition, sometimes perhaps more easily through poor ones than good ones. Finally, the tradition would mention a sense of enclosed spirits willfully cut off from their Creator that roam psychic and worldly space, diverting us from the truth of our souls, spirits that are called demonic.[8]

To me our ego/psychic structure is meant to be a precious vessel and an expression of the soul's life. However, we tend to make it an end in itself, which causes us to lose a sense of our larger soul-identity. Metaphorically speaking, we could say that in those times the psyche becomes a separated wanderer cut off in consciousness from its true Home. We become more self-protecting, grasping, and anxious as we identify with that fragile sense of little self. Both we and the world around us suffer accordingly. We need to embrace our deeper soul-identity, inviting the Spirit to lighten our little-self-absorption and leave us more available as vessels of God's loving Spirit.

This reorienting conversion process for most of us is a lifetime affair. Along the way we will likely discover that we go back and forth between identifying with a small, separated sense of self and with our deeper soul in God. Sometimes we will find that our identity with a small sense of self will lead us to use spirituality as a means of shoring up the fragile, small sense of self. For example, we can undertake a spiritual practice with the semiconscious intent of impressing others with what we've learned or of currying God's favor with our piety; or we can do a good deed in order to look good to ourselves or others. These intents leave our ego-identity in the driver's seat, where it wants to get something for itself. When we become aware of what we're doing, we might feel both tears of regret and a sense of gratitude that we've been "shown up," because that very awareness can be a grace that frees us to embrace more fully our deeper soul-identity in God. When that happens, we are more likely to pray or compassionately act in a way that lets our functional ego-self become a willing vessel of the Spirit.

We could apply here the adage, "Let go and let God": pray for the grace to let go of our overidentity with the grasping, fearing little-ego self, so that it can become not a deceptive locus of ultimate identity, but rather a willing vessel for God's Spirit ever alive in our deep souls, where our true identity lies.

Any attempt of our ego/psyche to possess the soul is doomed to failure. The soul cannot be possessed by the psyche. It does not belong to us. It belongs to God. Soul is not a self-contained box that we can possess. It is an orienting placeless place in our being where our spirit and God's Spirit live as almost-one. Our souls seem to trail off into God's being, so that it perhaps becomes impossible to say where we begin and God ends. God's energy seems all the way through us and through whatever happens.

If our freedom and what we do with it are what most define us as separate human beings, that separateness is relative to a larger connectedness with the Holy One. We could say that God's Spirit is present, alive, and moving inside our freedom, not just outside of it. God is hiddenly active though not controlling in our freedom. All of this is to say that there is an inexhaustible depth of Spirit running through us. No wonder scripture speaks of us as made in the image of God!

This image is hidden amidst the endless confusion that comes when we fall into an overly separated sense of ourselves, whether inspired by our own confusion and willfulness or by outside forces fallen away from God. But when the divine image appears in the manifest qualities of our inspired souls that I will speak of shortly, or even in our awareness that those qualities are there, however disempowered at the moment, then I think we are in touch with who we are at bottom. That in-touchness with our true nature in the divine image helps our psyches and bodies keep their honored place as carriers of Holy Spirit, rather than being seen as self-contained entities disconnected from that Spirit.

Such a disconnected sense of identity is dominant in our culture. That sense of disconnection easily leads to an impoverished, defensive view of ourselves and all of the sad fallout that results, both personally and societally. Jesus' good news is that we are truly larger than this view tells us. We are born of the divine Spirit, and that liberating Spirit is forever inviting and flashing our souls into fresh life.

We can understand here why spiritual disciplines arose historically. If we so easily miss our true identity in God and its calling in the moment, then we need some kind of ongoing practice that encourages the opening of our will and the appreciation of divine presence (I will return to this process in chapter four). When grace becomes appreciated and our identities have become more established in our deep souls in God, then we may be less in need of those disciplines. We live less attached to the "world," free to appreciate and care for it but not be owned by it. We live more spontaneously out of the grace at hand. But I think it is a very rare person, if anyone, who is fully stabilized in that larger identity in God. Most all of us need continual reminders of the Presence in the form of some ongoing practice and supportive spiritual community.

Some Qualities of Soul •

The fathomless mystery of soul manifests itself in certain qualities that reflect the divine nature, God's image, shining in us. I think we are born to show them forth in the particular Spirit-inspired forms and timings befitting the uniqueness of each one of us. I will name just seven of these qualities. It is far from a complete list; you may well think of others, or describe those I do mention in different terms.

Before naming them it is important to note that they are integrally related. They don't stand alone. Each one contains the seeds of the others. Watering one can help the others to show themselves. Starving one can hurt the others. They infuse one another in a myriad of ways. We could say that they are different outcroppings, different colorations, of the same divine loving energy of the Spirit at the core of our souls.

1. Spontaneous Compassion

Spontaneous compassion is different from a calculated attempt to love, be nice, be good, which is what we're left with when our souls are more filtered through our conditioned psyches. Spirit-inspired soul is showing itself most directly when it suddenly comes through as an uncalculated, sudden feeling or act of compassion in the moment. Our whole being flows into that compassion without calculation or hesitation. These pure moments of soulfullness carry with them a sense of simple confidence and of nonpossession. That is, we don't take credit for the feeling or act, because it is coming from that core of our souls where Merton said "God disposes of our lives." In that beautiful moment the Spirit is living *through* us, indeed, at its purest, we might say the Spirit is living *as* us.

These can be very simple moments almost unnoticed by us or others. They carry no ego-involved drama. They are loving, childlike events that Jesus I think would say reflect the "kingdom" of God among us (or the "kindom" of God, if we want to degender "kingdom"). If we image how love will be in heaven, I think we would portray it in this free form.

More effortful love, on the other hand, could be called the residue of the soul's spontaneous compassion in us. It is the memory of its importance, an echo of its free presence, an imitation of its ways. It is free love patterned into law and principled ethics. Such effortful love carries a certain suffering with it, because we instinctively know that the soul-fullness of loving is more free and direct.

It's important to note, though, that effortful loving is vital to human life and community. It is the basis of civil society together, at every level, from friendship and family to work, community, and politics. Such effortful love is all we seem capable of much of the time, and in that regard it could be considered part of the divine economy of things this side of heaven—it is the way life has been arranged. It is an indirect expression of soul and I think needs to be honored as such. Sometimes, though, a more direct compassion comes through us, an unmediated overflow of divine presence.

2. Freedom

Soul manifests itself as the freedom to move in any direction that may be called for. Such freedom leaves us lightly "poised" in the moment, not ultimately attached to anything, free for the call of the moment. Such freedom can be frightening in its unpredictability. Our confused, oversecuring psyches can resist such freedom both in ourselves and in others. It is not the same thing as impulsiveness, which is driven by inner psychic forces rather than by the call of the situation.

I think Jesus reflected this soul freedom in the way he was immediately available to the Holy Spirit in the many situations he found himself. We read of the fear that people had of him at times. I wonder if that fear stemmed in part from not being able to predict what Jesus was going to say or do in a given situation. A theologian once conjectured that Jesus never had a fixed identity; rather, he was always receiving who he was in each situation. He was directly available to be what was called for from that soul center in him where his spirit and God's Spirit were one.

3. Appreciation

Another quality of inspired soul is seen when we find ourselves appreciating the beauty and wonder inherent in a world soaked in mysterious divine energy, an appreciation which is an end-in-itself delight. Such appreciation can take the passive form of our being silently awestruck, or it can take an active form of our participation in the beauty and wonder through creative artistic acts, where we become artists of soul. Such appreciation shares the sheer ebullience of God in the endless creativity of marvelous dynamic forms and movements that the creation is.

Such appreciation contrasts with the numbness to beauty and wonder that is the bitter fruit of seeing things only in terms of their exploitable usefulness. Exclusively utilitarian values lead to the deadening commodification and finally the exhaustion of human and environmental resources. It drives us to overproductivity, because we no longer value the intrinsic worth and wonder of things, including our own intrinsic worth. We no longer value being with something or someone appreciatively just as they are in all their marvelous uniqueness. We lose the balance of active utilitarian creativity and receptive end-in-itself appreciation.

4. Awareness of Creation's Interwovenness

The soul can show an awareness of the intimate interwovenness of a creation all of whose forms and movements flow from the same divine Wellspring, in whom nothing is ultimately alien. We share a sense of cosmic family. Modern science reinforces this classically mystical awareness in the way it portrays the universe as a mysterious, dynamic, interrelated whole. For example, if we change the spin on one particle, another particle separated by whole galaxies somehow knows what has happened and reverses its spin instantaneously, using some form of communication faster than light. The meteorologist Edward Lorenz brings this interdependence down to earth when he says that the movement of a butterfly's wings in Tokyo ultimately affects the weather in New York.

This inspired sense of "interbeing" contrasts with the sense of isolation, overseparation, and exclusivity that appear when this quality of soul is hidden. We lose awareness of the inclusive community that deep spiritual traditions show us, which nonetheless can value the particularity of people and groups. For example, we can value the particularity of Christian community, yet we let that very particularity mediate a sense of connectedness to all that is in God. Jesus then is not the exclusive possession of Christians: Jesus belongs to God and to all that is of God. He draws us to be a priestly community that in a particular way mediates our universal connectedness, divine, human, and cosmic.

In the Eastern Orthodox tradition this community obliquely includes the personification of evil, Satan, whose reconciliation to God is prayed for, as I mentioned in the first chapter. In this way any ultimate dualism between good and evil is avoided. God is One in an inclusive community of creation, however wayward in its freedom elements of creation may be at a given time.

5. Holy Wisdom

Holy wisdom is a deep seeing of the truth and possibility of things. It is an inspired capacity for authentic sight, discernment, and hope. We all know those moments when we are suddenly free to see what is, and sometimes to see what can be and is meant to be. Such sight isn't necessarily accompanied by a clear cognitive understanding of such truth and hope. It is more of an intuitive seeing that spontaneously comes from beyond our figuring-out minds. It is what happens when the wind of the Spirit is blowing strongly in our soul's sails and we are just taken to an awareness of things. A larger wisdom shows itself in us, for which we cannot take the credit apart from a willingness to let the seeing and its fruits happen.

When this quality of soul is completely hidden, we are left with delusion and blindness. When it is partially hidden, when at least the desire to truly see is left in us, then it is equivalent to effortful compassion. We go through various steps of effortful discernment that take into consideration what the wisdom of the tradition and our own experience tell us about "holy seeing."

It is a little like putting on glasses when what we're seeing is a blur, and yet our sight is so bad that the glasses still don't bring us clear sight, just better sight. This is not the same as seeing with the clear, naked eye of the soul moved directly by the Spirit in a given situation. But at least effortful discernment gives us a way of expressing our desire for "holy seeing." And it gives us a way of staying within certain parameters that keep our seeing in the ballpark of the soul, however remotely.

6. Desire for the Allness of God

With John of the Cross we can say that all our desires finally are grounded in the foundational desire for the allness of God. All of our desires are sparks from the same divine hearth fire. Our souls show us this when our endless desires for loving, knowing, and unity find their orientation to the divine Lover, Knower, and Uniter who lives in our desires. Our souls eventually make us restless with any desire less than this fullness of communion with the One who mysteriously flows through all things.

When this foundational desire is hidden, we are left scattered amidst our myriad fragments of finite desires. They become like sparks that have lost their conscious connection with the fire that birthed them and lives in them. When the foundational desire for the allness of God is realized in us, then we taste something of the mystery of God's energy being within us in our soul's desire, reaching out for the fullness of God beyond us. We could say that we are a particular shaping of God's energy, magnetized to be drawn to its fullness in the vast intimacy of God beyond us. We hear this magnetism echoed in the opening of Psalm 42: "As a deer longs for flowing streams, so my soul longs for you, O God. My soul thirsts for God, for the living God."

7. Confident Trust

The last quality of soul I would hold up is an inspired confident trust—trust in a liberating, loving divine Presence available at the bottom of everything that is. When such trust streams through us, all the other qualities of soul I think have an easier time showing themselves. Sometimes we think of such trust as something we can make happen. We tell ourselves or others, "Just trust—just have faith." But we find out that it's not that easy. We can want it, hear inspiring things about it, pray for it, but lots of confused psychic forces in us conspire to punch holes in such trust and leave us really trusting only what we think we can control.

So, finally, real confident trust is a gift. As with compassion and holy wisdom, when such trust is not present spontaneously, we can put ourselves in its path through such means as inspirational reading about other people's trust, through prayer, and through expressing our desire for such trust with our spiritual director. Sometimes, though, the true fullness of trust does shine through; our whole being is pervaded by it. At its purest this is a "naked" trust, a trust that is beyond any particular content or object. The grace of such trust leaves us in amazement and thanksgiving.

In such qualities as these seven that I have briefly described, our souls indeed reflect God's Spirit in Christ alive in us. We could name other possible qualities of soul as well, including those behind the Beatitudes (Matt 5) and St. Paul's fruit of the Spirit (Gal 5:22ff.) to the degree that these are not already included implicitly in those I have chosen to identify.

I believe that this core dimension of our true identity and being, our soul, can interact with other souls at a level deeper than our conditioned psyches. Each such exchange reverberates the divine blessing among us. We are a community of souls through which divine radiance expresses itself in ever fresh ways. Brother Lawrence of the Resurrection said that we would be surprised to know what our souls are saying to God. I would expand this to say that we would be surprised to know what our souls are saying to one another. So much of our deepest communication is only vaguely perceptible to our minds.

We belong together in God at a far deeper level than our normal consciousness comprehends. This is the basis for what I will be saying in chapter six about the importance of the director's and directee's contemplative quality of presence to one another, inviting as much of a God-to-soul and soul-to-soul communication as possible. Such a quality of presence helps us be available for the psalmist's experience where he says, "I bless Yahweh, who is my counselor, and in the night my inmost self instructs me" (Ps 16:7 JB).

Examining Your Own Soul Callings •

You might find it valuable, with or without a spiritual companion, to reflect on your experience of these and perhaps other inspired qualities of soul. Such reflection may help you to appreciate some of the Spirit's activity in your life. You may sense a calling to some particular quality of soul that is being empowered at this point in your life, for which you can offer thanks and willing dedication.

You may notice a sense of resistance to letting yourself identify with your deep soul in God and its callings. Identification with our deep souls leaves our ego-level identity as a trusting servant of soul rather than its master. Such trust is not always empowered in us. The resulting resistance can be opened to God in prayer, where we can ask for the freedom to trust and serve the movements of God's life in us, for our own sake and for the sake of God's kindom in the world.

CHAPTER 3

HOW DO WE KNOW? THE NATURE OF SPIRITUAL EXPERIENCE

When directees come into spiritual direction sessions and speak about particular experiences that to them reflects God's activity in their lives, it can be helpful to be aware of the different ways our minds are conscious of such experiences. "Knowing," in its largest sense, refers to the variety of ways we experience life, as well as how we appreciate and interpret our experience. As such, it includes but is not limited to our cognitive activity.

In a broad sense we can see every experience we have as a spiritual experience, insofar as we believe that God's Spirit is intimately involved with all that happens in life. More specifically, however, we can see spiritual experiences as events that have a particular capacity to show us the nature and guidance of God in our souls and in life around us.

In scripture such "showings" of God's presence are seen as a result of God's loving, transforming activity with us that awakens recognition of grace, responsive loving, and faith. These showings therefore give us a kind of spiritual knowledge that is not a speculative, detached, once-and-for-all knowledge of eternal verities. Rather, it is a knowledge that is the fruit of ongoing divine initiative and active human response. It involves a dynamic process of realizing the truth and calling of our being and community in God.

Such faith-knowledge can show itself at all the levels of touching an experience that will be described below. What we have received and embraced of this faith-knowledge is the ground of our willing presence for God through all the ways we touch experience. This thread of active orientation to God woven through all dimensions of our knowing I will later describe under the heading of "prayerful presence."

Below you will find a simple diagram that summarizes one way of looking at the levels of knowing human experience that has grown from my personal understanding.

"PRAYERFUL PRESENCE" through All Ways of Knowing

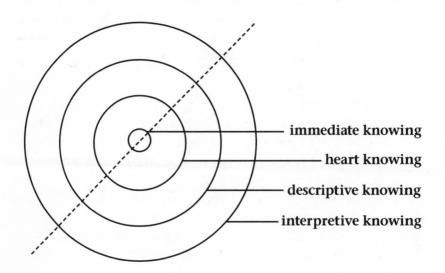

- immediate knowing
- heart knowing
- descriptive knowing
- interpretive knowing

An Experience of Your Own •

You probably will find my descriptions of each of these levels of knowing easier to understand if you will take the time to answer these two questions about a concrete experience of your own.

1. Try to recall some simple way that you have been aware of the Spirit's presence in the past month, even if that presence was noticeable only through some moment of your desire for it (I'm assuming that the desire itself is a movement of the Spirit). What are the indicators that lead you to sense that this really was the Spirit's direct presence rather than something more physiologically or psychologically derived, or demoniacally related (demonic in the sense of something that can destructively capture your total spirit rather than lovingly liberate it)? Examples of a few possible indicators of direct divine presence might be one or more of the following:
   a. the fruits of the experience, such as a sense of deep peace, liberation from sin or illusion, reconciliation, fresh sense of mission;
   b. the experience did not seem to rise out of or serve my ego's controlling nature, but rather appeared to come from a deeper soul-place;
   c. an opening-to-God experience shared by others.

2. See if you can be in touch with some of the widening circles of consciousness related to the experience. You may not have an association with all of those that follow—they can all be present within a few seconds of time in an experience. Often we have no special awareness of the first three circles.
   a. a sense of radiant reality on the horizon of awareness which is so "intimate" that there is no sense of subject or object distinction;

b. your spiritual heart's obscure sense of a benevolent presence (at this point you sense some difference from, yet personal unity with, this larger presence);

c. your images or words that describe this dawning sense of friendly presence;

d. a sense of interpretation of the experience (e.g., this seems like an experience of God showing end-in-itself love; and/or something God is showing me to be or do);

e. your response to this sense of presence (e.g., awe, thanksgiving, repentance, love, embracing or resisting a sense of call, disorientation);

f. a sense of some way it connects with scripture, tradition, and past personal experience;

g. any further conscious fruits of this experience in your inner or outer life.

I suggest that you keep this concrete example in mind now as I explain these dimensions of touching an experience. I will thread a simple example of my own throughout these descriptions. As I said above, in practice all of these levels of knowing may happen within a few seconds of time. Often we may not be aware of more than one of them, in which case we may be missing a fuller possible understanding of what is being given us in an experience.

The Dawning of Awareness

We begin with the edge of mystery, because anything coming to us from the beyondness of God has an origin that is deeper than our minds can take us. The beginning of our experience thus is shrouded in darkness. Whatever we can know at that deepest place we know not through our cognitive thinking but through our spiritual hearts (the subtly conscious dimension of our souls) or through the even greater immediacy of our contemplative intuition (our capacity for direct, unitive involvement).

Heart Knowing

Let me speak first about the spiritual heart, the second circle on the diagram, since that is a little easier for us to grasp than the first circle of immediate knowing, contemplative intuition. My spiritual heart, for example, can sense a friendly force in and around me that feels real beyond the construction of my ego's need or imagination. When this spiritual sense is operational, I feel myself in a spontaneous, conscious relationship with this benevolent force.

The relationship at this level of knowing is so intimate that at its purest I can sense the relationship itself to be more substantial than any sense of a separate personal self. When later my reflective thinking capacity becomes operational and I am able to use words to try and describe this level of contact with the experience, I might use words like, "It seemed as though I was a kind of glow from that deep reality, a particular shaping of its loving creativity," or I might use many other ways to describe what it was like.

As a more specific example of an identified spiritual experience, I may have a sudden interior opening that my spiritual heart senses as an overwhelming love. I seem so much part of that love that I barely distinguish a separate "me" from it; I and everything seem part of that love. Even so, I do distinguish my separateness. This heart sense does have a certain quality of feeling and personal identity.

Immediate Knowing

What I call immediate knowing, or, alternatively, contemplative intuition, the inmost circle on the diagram, does not even have these minimal senses of personal separateness. This is a dimension of awareness found in contemplative tradition that is not usually even identified outside this tradition, and so it is not easy to grasp, even though it inherently belongs to all of us. It is implied in the writings of great Western mystics, but it is more carefully and systematically recognized in certain strands of Asian traditions that cultivate precise mental awareness of the mind's activity involved in spiritual experience.[1]

Contemplative intuition is the most direct way of knowing, unconditioned by our thinking, feeling, symbols, heart senses, or past experience. It is a quality of open consciousness that exists before these become operational in our minds. Before any of these arise, there is a direct in-touchness with "what is." This immediate in-touchness carries its own knowledge unmediated by any of these normal conditioners of consciousness. There is no separation of subject and object, no delineation of self and other. Rather, there is a pristine, unitive awareness, a quality of radiant, inclusive presence. We are in the stream of reality-as-it-is very directly, with no sense of personal possession. When this way of knowing occurs during prayer, then we no longer even know we are praying. Any sense of definition of "I" is suspended.

It might be helpful to an understanding of what it's like to have no separate sense of "I" to write in your journal with no possessive pronouns. For example, instead of saying, "I am writing in my journal," you would say, "Pen moves over paper." Even this sentence isn't fully adequate for our purposes, since, even though it does not define a separate sense of self, it is too full of other definitions like "pen" and "paper," than would be true when we are purely present in the stream of reality-as-it-is. That is more like being part of a happening without defining forms. And yet the forms are there without names. It isn't just a blur. Everything is present as it is before our definitions of forms and before our singling ourselves out as a possessor of the forms.

Another exercise that might help you better sense this quality of presence would be to let yourself follow the second hand of a clock, giving up any labeling of "clock," "second hand," "self watching." Your eyes just simply join the movement of that second hand. When you drop the labels the distance between you and the second hand collapses. You are "in" the second hand, so to speak, until you separate yourself "out" the moment you start labeling things.

Ironically enough, while you are watching the clock, a human-made version of sequential time, your consciousness enters a more inclusive, nonlinear time. It accommodates infinitely more than the restrictive consciousness involved when you single yourself out as an observer of what is happening and label the clock as a clock. When these are let go, your consciousness becomes more open. There is an awareness of everything present as it is, which is experienced as a vibrant, multidimensional reality much vaster than the one perceived when we keep a strong subject-object separation. You become aware of a quality of knowing that is inherent in the appearances, so that you do not need to step outside of it in order to know. It is a radically different quality of knowing.

This quality of awareness exists in the split second before some image of self rises to try and "possess" it as a separate self. Once we begin to sense a self in relation to this awareness, we have moved to what I call the spiritual heart's sensing capacity, that second circle on the diagram, about which I have already spoken. That capacity is grounded in this direct quality of in-touchness with what is, but it adds a sense of self and, with it, a certain vague sense of defined objects apart from the self.

In certain particularly graced times, out of this first circle's stream of immediate presence, we might find particular words or actions spontaneously arising that bypass our interpretive thinking and sometimes even bypass our heart sensing. For example, in the experience of love that I earlier mentioned, this level of immediate knowing would be there for a split second before I sensed what I am calling "love." In that flash of time I would be so given to the communing love at the heart of reality, so unseparated from it, that in God's empowering grace I would become a direct expression of that love.

If I were in a spiritual direction session at the time, out of such a direct awareness I might suddenly express something of the nature of love that comes from beyond my normal mediated consciousness. This could take the form of anything from a particularly loving way of looking at the person, to particular words concerning love relevant to what that directee has been saying, to words or a gesture that on the surface may seem unconnected with what went before. The evidence that this spontaneous, uncalculated expression was in some way indicative of God's Spirit rather than some other force might be seen in its fruits: in the spiritually positive effect of this expression on the directee, in the session or sometime afterward.

My belief is that unitive awareness is available to everyone all the time. It is that wide-eyed, inclusive, open awareness available for a flash between every thought, a quality that I think we glimpse in that deep, open looking we sometimes see in the eyes of very young children. However, since in the cultures that I know we normally only notice experiences that include a strong sense of self-definition and reflective thought, this quality of awareness and its fruits easily escape us as a recognized reality.

Especially when we are in spiritual direction, we can desire that our presence be grounded in such precognitive intimacy with the larger Presence whom we trust is radiantly at work in our midst. This desire can lead us to let our minds be open and "unknowing" when we are with a directee, wanting God to be known as God wants to be known, through and between us. We can invite that Presence to slip in between our thoughts with liberating, guiding, loving wisdom. This stance of immediate open presence for God will be emphasized in various ways again and again in this book. As implied earlier, it is foundational to the deeper spiritual life and to spiritual companionship.

Descriptive Knowing *the edge/end of ineffability?*

A beginning sense of self-definition occurs, as I implied earlier, when our heart sense identifies what is happening as belonging to "me," even though this sense of me still feels intimately a part of the experience itself. We then bring into operation our cognitive, categorizing faculty of knowing when we move beyond the heart sense of the experience to the use of descriptive images in order to make the experience more accessible to our reflective mind. This happened earlier when I described the experience to be "as though I was a kind of glow from that deep reality, a particular shaping of a loving creativity."

Such analogies move us beyond the purity of our immediate experience. As a result we might say that by the time we have become conscious of our experience it has become an experience of an experience. Our minds have constructed an image of a reality that in itself is happening before our normal mental apparatus becomes operational to describe it, and that descriptive capacity can never do it full justice.

Sometimes the descriptive image that comes to us is very sharp and concrete, as in the appearance of symbols and of holy beings like Jesus or Mary. We may sense that these images mirror a true divine message for us that is beyond our subjective fantasizing. Because the origin and meaning of these images remain deeper than our capacity to understand them fully, we need a certain humility when we move beyond describing what they were like to interpreting their meaning for us or for others. As with the "showings" of the medieval anchoress Julian of Norwich, it may be many years after their appearance before their fuller meaning is given to us, or it may never be given us.

If the appearance is truly of God, though, and we are truly wanting God rather than self-aggrandizement, then I think whatever we really need to learn from it will be given us in God's own time. We do not have to try and force an understanding with our cognition. We can simply maintain, as Julian exhorted, an ongoing, light, alert sensitivity and desire for truth to show itself as we are ready for and needful of it. With John of the Cross we can also be confident that God can work effectively in us secretly, without our always having to be given conscious knowledge of it. This trust can leave us that much freer from the temptation to try and force a conscious understanding.

Interpretive Knowing

When we move beyond a simple description of an immediate, heart-sensed experience into interpretation of where it comes from, what it means, and how it relates to others' experience historically and today, we become theologians. For example, once we use the name "God" in relation to our experience, we are making a theological statement. When I go beyond describing my experience of an overwhelming sense of love to say that it is an experience of *God's* love, I have moved beyond immediate description of the experience itself to a faith statement about the source of the experience. Theologians in this sense are people who take seriously and reflect prayerfully on the meaning of what they identify as their own active, direct spiritual experience.

Historically this normally would be done in the light of reason, our own past experience, the experience and interpretations found in scripture, the testimony of the great saints, and perhaps the great councils and writings of the church, depending on our particular tradition. Besides this historical communal context, such theologizing could involve a *current* communal context, reflecting on the communal experience of a group of people who are seeking to discern God's guiding hand in their experience.

This understanding of theologizing, where we stay close to lived experience, is what we are most concerned with in spiritual direction. More specifically, we are concerned with what is called spiritual theology as opposed to those forms of theology that operate at a more abstract and generalized level of interpretation and integration. These latter forms provide a broad context for looking at our experience, but they are not specifically geared to attending our experience.

Spiritual theology at its purest involves reflection on the ways images, thoughts, feelings, and movements of will that rise from our prayerful presence show us something about our communion and calling in God, including callings to particular spiritual practices. Thus spiritual theologizing is happening whenever we attempt to understand the particular ways God seems to personally move in and among us, inviting us into a realization of our communion and into compassionate, creative callings flowing from that communion. Spiritual theologizing also involves noticing and dealing with counterinvitations: those that emanate from ego centeredness, debilitating societal forces, and forces of evil.

Each of us has a lot of assumptions about the nature of God, persons, and tradition that affect the way we interpret what is happening to us and others. Sometimes these theological assumptions may be hidden from our consciousness. We need to be open to exposing and testing their adequacy for consonance with our actual experience and with the fullness and ongoing dialogue of the tradition.

Albert Einstein once said that "it is the theory which decides what we can observe." Our theological assumptions are the theories, if you will, that allow either a narrow or broad, a distorted or truer interpretation of experience for ourselves and for others.

Continuing with my earlier example of an overwhelming experience of love, when I begin "knowing" that experience in the context of Judeo-Christian tradition, I might interpret it as a way God is directly showing me the loving communion that exists between us. I might also see it as an invitation and empowerment to deepen my own responsive love for God. I might further find in it an invitation and empowerment for some particular way of loving God's creatures in light of my life circumstances and gifts. (This might not show itself immediately after the experience, but become evident sometime later.)

All of these interpretations reflect ones that can be found in scripture and tradition. However, a number of interpretations of any given experience may be possible, so we need to be careful not to lock in on one interpretation prematurely. We need to remember Julian's advice not to force a particular interpretation.

The spiritual director can be helpful in avoiding premature closure of interpretation by the directee. This openness can be helped by being sure that the descriptive level of knowing is not bypassed, as can easily happen. At the descriptive level there remains a sense of greater closeness to the actual experience and openness concerning its possible meanings. Having said this, though, it is important not to become caught up in an overly detailed and analytical approach to the experience. What is most important, I think, is prayerfully listening to the basic impact of the experience on the directee. What does it seem to be doing to their sense of God and themselves?

The Interaction of the Ways We Know Spiritual Experience

Before the interpretive level of knowledge, as we have seen, there is the level of simple description of experience. Before this there is a kind of simple, childlike heart-knowledge, the kind of underlying inner sense we can have when we are praying. At this level of the spiritual heart we sense a quality of desire, presence, trust, and love that carries an obscure yet substantial knowledge of a larger caring reality. Our interpretive knowledge can help give us more confidence to take seriously this level of knowing, for example, by saying that God is the real subject of our experience. Further, I think our interpretation has its way of affecting the way we are present at this heart-level, for example, interpreting that God unconditionally loves us can leave us freer to be vulnerable and open.

Our heart-knowledge in turn affects our interpretive theologizing. For example, God is sensed as a liberating presence, leading us to interpret God as liberator. In spiritual direction we need to stay close to this heart-level of knowing and our descriptions of it. When we are at the interpretive theological level, we need to let it be illuminated by our heart-knowledge. At all times we need to remain open to those intuitive contemplative flashes, our "immediate knowing," where our own and God's energy are free to live with a particular shared immediacy. These flashes in turn need to be verified in terms of their loving fruits as understood in scripture, tradition, and our own experience.

Summary of the Dimensions of Knowing a Spiritual Experience •

Whatever our theological assumptions at a given time, they reflect an interpretive knowledge that surrounds our descriptive knowledge and our more childlike, obscure-to-the-intellect knowledge of the spiritual heart. This heart-knowledge in turn surrounds our direct, pristine, pure spiritual presence that involves a more immediate quality of objectless knowledge where there is no separation of subject and object; this is the un-self-possessed "knowingness" of unitive awareness. Each of these circles of knowing radiating out from the experience itself reflects some dimension of the soul, that ineffable essence of our being where God's Spirit in Christ lives in us, calling us into fullness of life.

Prayerful Presence

The dotted diagonal line running through the circles-of-knowing diagram displayed earlier refers to the possibility of prayerful presence through all of the circles. All of these dimensions of knowing can be pervaded by a way of being willingly present for God and trusting God's presence for us. This is an orientation, a stance of our whole being, which encompasses whatever way we are knowing at a given time. It will not be conscious at the immediate level of knowing, since we are not consciously willing anything then, yet even that level can be undergirded by a prior desire for whatever might happen in such a time to be guided by God's presence, as well as any later reflection on its fruits.

Such an open, trusting, willing presence for God's loving truth, or at least the desire for such presence, can be seen as the essence of a contemplative orientation at every level of knowing. It can be lost when we "lean forward" too graspingly in our interpretive knowledge and lose its immediate openness to God. Our knowing then tends to become more insular, feeding on itself, so to speak, one concept growing out of another, without being rooted in our desire for immediate presence to God.

We are conditioned to this insularity at every level of our educational system, so it takes great conscious attentiveness to let our thoughts grow out of and feed into our immediate givenness to God. We will often fail, but at least we can be aware of the "lost connection" after a while, and then return to it. This connectedness, which we will return to in chapter six, is particularly crucial for the spiritual director.

Theology and the Mystery of God •

One purpose of theology is to honor, at the interpretive level, the full mystery of God and of our own nature in the image of God. Such an intent helps to keep our interpretations humbly open to the subtlety, largeness, and directness of spiritual reality. At the same time, theology helps us to recognize the consistent core of the Gospel, the Good News of God's liberating love that has been revealed in Christ, scripture, creation, and human history.[2]

Since our theologizing is relative to a mystery that transcends our understanding, we can have honest differences of interpretation with one another. When we gather together in a direction session to probe this deep divine mystery that we sense is at work in us, we can trust that where two or three are gathered together in true willingness for God, Christ's Spirit will guide us, even if our probing leaves us at different places of understanding and confusion at a given time.

Another dimension of knowing worth touching upon concerns the Christian traditions of *kataphatic* and *apophatic* ways of approaching spiritual knowledge. The *kataphatic* underlines positive images of God, expressing the human capacity to reach God through forms: creatures, images, and symbols. The *apophatic,* on the other hand, calls all particular human expressions of God radically inadequate. God is "not this, not that." God is imagelessly known in the spaces between and behind the forms.

One advantage of marrying these approaches rather than making them a mutually contradictory choice is that we become a little less tempted to insist on the ultimately right words and answers to things with our cognitive minds, while still valuing those minds for what comes through them. For example, the *apophatic* assumption that God is always more than any images we may have of the divine frees us for a naked, imageless trust that is open and spacious. We can trust that God is at work in us in a hidden way that we do not have to understand in order for that divine work to be operative. At the same time, the *kataphatic* assumption that God comes to us through manifest forms, human and otherwise, allows us to appreciate God's presence through all the concrete forms of life that we encounter.

When both these approaches are appreciated, God's active presence is realized to pervade both our knowing and our unknowing, the forms of life and the spaces between them, the sounds and the silences. Then it is a little easier to both appreciate our knowing through forms and yet not to press our knowing beyond its limits at a given time. It is all right to see through a glass darkly, not to understand clearly.

The classic holy icon, so prevalent in Eastern Orthodox traditions and increasingly appreciated in Western churches, is a fine example of the marriage of *kataphatic* and *apophatic* understandings. The reverenced form (the painted image) of the icon shows appreciation for the incarnate presence of God's Spirit. At the same time, the theological understanding that the icon's image draws us through and beyond itself to the invisible mystery of divine presence shows appreciation for God's reality beyond what the mind can grasp.[3]

Discernment •

The ways of knowing a spiritual experience can provide a helpful experiential foundation for approaching discernment in a spiritual direction relationship. When someone comes to us seeking God's will, in the light of God's love for them and for creation and in the light of their own experience, we are involved in a process of discernment. Such a process in a Christian context assumes the twofold vocation that I have earlier mentioned: to be in love, and to overflow that love; to ever more deeply realize loving union and to live out of that union in the community of creation.

Discernment as an ongoing daily *habit* involves living from a trust in God's abiding, loving presence every moment and from a willingness to habitually turn to God's Spirit in our souls and rest openly there, wanting to be free to move in any direction that Love shows us. Discernment as a specific *act,* where we are seeking God's will related to a specific question of calling, grows out of that same habitual stance of open presence. How is the Spirit drawing us in a particular direction? How do our deep desires, opened to God, and our deep listening show us something of that movement in our souls?

The desert fathers and mothers were often involved in such discernment, *diakrisis,* seeking what in our interior movements was of God, of ego-self, or of demonic spirits (which were seen as often working through connivance with our ego distortions, such as greed and distrust). There is a long history of discernment stretching behind the desert tradition to scriptural sources and through the patristic, medieval, and modern periods of church history.[4] A recurring theme is attention to the fruit of an inner movement. If the movement is good, then the inner response and outer results will be good (though not necessarily painless!).

St. Paul's list of the fruit of the Spirit (Gal 5:22ff.), in contrast with the fruit of the bad spirit (the "flesh") (Gal 5:19–21), is central to the tradition. Authentic gifts of the Spirit for Paul are marked by light, peace, charity, and humility that spread to the community. The First Letter of John encourages us not to believe every spirit but to test them to see whether they are from God (4:1). Elsewhere St. Paul sets up the standard of continuity with past normative experiences of the church: Authentic revelation harmonizes with or deepens a revelation already confided.

Such a standard has helped guard a sense of human unity in spiritual knowledge, a standard that helps in countering oversubjective illuminations that leave people more vulnerable to Jonestowns and other self-styled religious cults. Of course, if "revelation already confided" is interpreted too narrowly, as it frequently has been, then the opposite danger of enforced, sterile conformity is at hand. The First Letter of John helps to counter this danger in its assertion that anointing of the Spirit gives certitude and light independent of any human teachings.[5] The whole prophetic tradition weighs in here, as well: Prophets, through inspiration of the Holy Spirit, challenge false conformities and injustice and raise up the divine loving call to authentic holiness and shalom in individuals and in the community. Jesus himself expresses this prophetic call continually.

St. Ignatius Loyola, in the sixteenth century, provided a practical method that shifted the weight of earlier discernment tradition away from examining our attitudes, virtues, sins, and general state of life to looking at our actions. He asked what the Spirit was calling us to do, not only what we were to be, which would orient our lives in concrete situations "to the glory and praise of God."

A highlight of Ignatius's many contributions is his sense of the three good times for vocational decision making:

1. when our will is moved to a point where no hesitation is possible;
2. when we find light and information through reflection on our experiences of desolation (darkness, turmoil, sloth, tepidness, etc.) and consolation (movements tending toward faith, hope, love, peace, etc.);
3. in a period of calm, when the soul is not agitated by diverse spirits and exercises its natural faculties freely and tranquilly.

Ignatius suggests ways of enhancing the validity of this third decision-making way, including deciding as though you were at the moment of death or by picturing an unknown person you would like to see practice perfection: How would s/he decide?[6] We could add to these: remembering an earlier time in our lives when we sensed God's loving presence and call amidst our openness. Which of the choices before me now seems most congruent with this deepest sense of God?

The discernment and other spiritual practices of Ignatius were spread widely in the Roman Catholic world after his death. Since the Second Vatican Council they have undergone a renaissance of interest and modification, and they have been spilling over into the Protestant world. I doubt that any other single approach to discernment has had so much written about it. Many of these recent Ignatian-inspired writings have made a significant contribution to an understanding and practice of discernment. An Ignatian-based understanding is a basic dimension of many spiritual direction programs.[7] However, in the hands of many of its interpreters it tends toward a rationally structured process that has a very different flavor than the more direct, intuitive, charismatic, "shocking" style preserved from the desert, as we see for example in Eastern Orthodox writers.[8] Some people are more attracted to this style than to a normal Ignatian approach. I don't think the essence of either style need contradict the other, nor need they become exclusive choices. Both may have their authentic time in a given person's life.

Perhaps in the West we come closest to this simpler second discernment style in the corporate and individual discernment practices of the Society of Friends (Quakers). At their best they reflect the gentle, stable domesticity of medieval and later English spirituality, together with a subtle attunement to "the Light within," seeking mutual edification from the movements of this Light arising in shared silence.[9]

Such simplicity in approaching the Spirit's movements upholds those qualities of presence that I began to unfold at the start of this section: a habitual leaning into our souls in God, with a quality of trust in the abyss of divine love there, wanting to see our desires transformed in the light of God's desire for us. We rest attentively in that abyss ultimately without knowing anything except our desire to embody those qualities of soul in our lives that I mentioned in the last chapter, especially at this point that quality which I called "Holy Wisdom," a deep seeing of the truth and possibility of our life in God. As I stated earlier, when the wind of the Spirit is blowing strongly in us, we are just taken to an awareness of things, as in the first time for vocational decision making mentioned by St. Ignatius.

But more often we are not given such clear sight and rest in our trust that we will be given enough of what we need to see as we go along. Our temptation is to try and force this sight, to separate from the Presence and try to figure out things on our own, forcing a premature decision. Sometimes decisions need to be made without clear sight, but with just enough light to take a first step in one direction or another, trusting that the Spirit will shape our path with us as we go along.

In terms of the spiritual path in general, I believe that there is no preplanned path for us. Our unique path is formed with each step we take. God does not seem to have a blueprint for our lives. Divine guidance is more of an always-emerging, spontaneous happening, full of divine freedom and love, fully attuned to our loved nature and situation. This is consonant with Thomas Merton's view of the ongoing "improvisation" of the Spirit in our lives. What we can do in a discernment process above all is maintain our trusting desire for the fullness of life for ourselves and for the world in God, our desire to join God's desire for life and to let whatever our minds do by way of reflection on our calling be in the context of claiming that desire.

This process may well not provide clear specific discernment, but over time I think it can provide a way of approaching decisions that frees us from a focus on "getting it right," that is, finding out just what God wants, or else we will be lost. Instead, we become free for a focus on an ongoing divine/human dance together that is less concentrated on right answers than on a right inner orientation, one that keeps us living out of our deep souls no matter how vague our sense of what decision to make. Then we are living more by steady trust than by demanded sight. Perhaps our minds always want to see more than they really need to see. When we live out of our souls in trust, we become looser about knowing, and willing for a blind walk when that is what is given.

The spiritual direction session offers a space where both directee and director can claim their desire for the larger Love that invites our trust and not our fearful forcing of things. In the presence of the director's desire for that creative Love to live as fully as possible in the directee, the directee may relax enough so that s/he sinks back more easily into that Presence in their souls where they realize they are not on their own. From that place, shared by director and directee, listening can lead to surprising glimpses of grace and sometimes of clearer direction for life.

The director sits in quiet confidence that the directee will be given what needs to be known and not given what doesn't need to be known at this moment. The director doesn't try to force clarity, but models a deep, trusting, listening presence that is content with what is given as enough for now. This can take great patience and resistance to the temptation to satisfy the directee's desire for answers when none have been authentically given.

The director can also help a person to look carefully at an experience or sense of direction, to sift through the different ways of knowing, as illustrated in the diagram earlier in this chapter, helping the directee notice the difference between the experience itself and his or her heart senses, descriptions, and interpretations of it. This may not be needed in most cases, but where, for example, the director senses that the directee has jumped too quickly to an interpretation of an experience and its life implications, some questioning may be helpful.

When a directee has been moved to a particular significant decision, it needs time to be confirmed in the following weeks or months, in accord with the long tradition of looking at the fruits of our decisions. Denis Edwards helpfully describes this process:

> As we go about our daily duties and face difficulties in life, what is truly of God will find confirmation in a sense of deep peace in God, in spite of external complexities. The decision we have made will need to find confirmation in its actual effects. This means that the

way it affects others, and what it opens up in us, will be experienced as of God.[10]

Sometimes the director can help the directee notice the psychic barriers to discernment that may show themselves (without playing psychotherapist and trying to help the directee psychologically analyze and cope with them). These can include a wide range of fears, scars, willfulness, and illusory views that impede the directee's freedom to move in certain directions. Prayer can be offered for the release of these "unfreedoms," as well as for an acceptance of their limitations to the extent that they remain present in the person's life. In some cases we might suggest psychological help. We can still want God despite and even through those unfreedoms, or at least *want* to want God.

Extraordinary Prayer Experiences •

The director also may be called upon to look with the directee at "extraordinary" prayer experiences, such as visions, voices, or speaking in tongues. The great articulator of deep contemplative life, John of the Cross, has a sustained discussion of such phenomena in 2:16–32 of *The Ascent of Mount Carmel.* He basically views them as potentially of God, but he sees them as too remote a means of union. They can lead us to God, but they are not God. They can be appreciated, but basically should be ignored in favor of a shorter and surer path to God: the path of dark contemplative faith.

For the soul and divine wisdom to be united, they will have to come to accord by means of a certain likeness. As a result the soul must also be pure and simple, unlimited and unattached to any particular knowledge, and unmodified by the boundaries of form, species, and image.[11]

In line with John's understanding, the director might help the directee to lightly appreciate any phenomenon, but not to dwell on or become fascinated with it. What has shown itself is an experience along the way. God's presence may flash through it, but union with God is found in our reflection of those qualities of God that John mentioned, which involves not being focused upon any particular form or knowledge. Denis Edwards adds this insight to the subject:

> There is no way of knowing when a person has been guided by the Holy Spirit in the whole process of enfleshing the experience of God, except by the results and the fruits of what is expressed. What is clear both in theory and from many practical cases is that a person may be quite holy and apparently enjoying genuine experience of God and yet have visions or hear words that are quite erroneous.
>
> John of the Cross has provided us with a practical approach to these phenomena. We are always to turn our heart back to a stance of openness and waiting for the gift of God given in the darkness of faith, rather than to go seeking after such experiences which are byways from the path which leads directly to God.[12]

Shift in the Locus of Discernment •

Roman Catholic, Anglican, and mainstream Protestant church practice of spiritual direction today, at least in Western countries, has largely veered away from obedience to the spiritual guide in the old absolutist sense. Currently, in the practice of most directors in these churches, the final locus of discernment as to what is happening and called for in the directee's spiritual life has shifted from the director to the directee, or to a kind of mutual discernment between them. Also, the director for a monk or a seminarian today tends to be someone other than the legal superior of the community, allowing the relationship to evolve in a more equal fashion.

The directors in these modern contexts listen with the directee for what God's Spirit seems to be up to, asking probing questions, perhaps offering suggestions, and above all providing a supportive, prayerful presence for deep listening. They see themselves at most as codiscerners with directees. In the end it is the directees who need to own the discernment as truly theirs and carry out its implications as they are moved to do so, rather than because they have been told to do so. The spiritual director of today, then, is rarely an authoritative figure, but one who humbly prays, probes, and listens for the directions of the Spirit with a fellow spiritual pilgrim.

Perhaps the closest historical precedent for this more humble role of the director as it relates to discernment is found in the nonauthoritarian "clearness committee" of the Society of Friends, where a group of people come together to help a person probe what the Holy Spirit is calling forth. The early Methodist band also seemed to reflect some elements of this mutual probing that respects the individual's final discernment. A variety of other Protestant group meetings probably included such elements as well, together with countless anonymous, informal, occasional spiritual friendships.

Beyond Discernment •

In accounts of the deeper spiritual life we find descriptions of the rare person who has been graced to truly become given and transparent to the divine Presence in a fairly steady way. Bernard of Clairvaux speaks of the spiritual life in terms of four stages of love: the love of ourselves, the love of God for our own sake, the love of God for God's sake, and the love of ourselves for God's sake.[13] Beginning in the third stage, where we are graced to love God for God's sake, we have moved from the consolations of God to an identity with the God of consolations. At that point we can understand the wisdom of St. Augustine's advice to "love God and do what you will." Arrival at these stages does not mean that one has realized union with God, but the ground for union seems more fertile. As that union shows itself, the normal means of discernment seem to disappear. People at this point no longer struggle with discernment. They act from their souls without calculation. Life happens out of their healed, whole relationship with God, in God. They do what they do with simplicity, fearlessness, and full givenness to God, in an intimacy that goes beyond even needing to name God. All the qualities of soul I mentioned are manifest as called for. Their very being in such times becomes a spontaneous capacity for God.

In the fullness of that union they have moved from the image of God in which they were born, to the likeness of God in which they truly realize that image in them—the realized union of God's Spirit with our spirit, of Christ's nature with our nature. They say with the great mystics then that all is grace, that God alone lives for them in and through all things, that they exist in and for that great Love. They have been willing for and graced with John of the Cross's dark night of the senses and the spirit,[14] and they have been brought to the radiant, buoyant dawn of union beyond. They have burned with the divine purging heat until there is nothing left but the lightness of their shape glowing in the divine Fire.

I have never known any living human being who manifests such a realization for more than a brief time. What makes a mystical saint, I believe, is the graced capacity for a more sustained realization than that which happens for others. Speaking personally, there is the desire in me to be with someone who manifests such realized union more steadily. As a Christian, this desire feeds my personal relationship with Jesus Christ as one who shows this God-given realization and offers a living, guiding relationship unbounded by time and space.

My sense is that everyone, over the years of an intentional spiritual journey, has moments of such realized union, moments that perhaps we don't even remember, because there is so little of "us" in them. But we easily fall back into a heavier and plodding sense of self. I myself yearn to realize that union more steadily, despite my trepidation about losing my known self in the process, the heavy little self with which I still often identify. I believe this yearning is a divinely planted seed hidden in all of us. At the same time, it is important to trust that the union is already present, whether realized by us or not, and that our lives and the world are full of grace in every moment, however hidden to our consciousness.

In spiritual direction the director, the directee, or both together may taste flashes of union and spontaneous discernment. In those moments we find manifest some aspect of the kindom of heaven, the reign of God, the deep life of our souls in Christ. In such times there is nothing to do but accept the gifted moment with simple gratitude and pray for it to bear fruit in our lives and the life of the world. When these moments recede and we are left with a greater sense of separateness, we can let the memory of such times stoke our deep desire for the full realization of our life and the world's life in God.

CHAPTER 4

WHAT DO WE DO?
THE NURTURE OF SOUL

Spiritual direction doesn't stand in isolation as an arena for the soul's nurture. It is surrounded and supported by a host of other potentially nurturing practices that may be reflected upon in the spiritual direction relationship, in terms of how they draw us toward or away from our true self and community in God. Besides individual and collective practices, spiritual direction also takes place in the context of different spiritual paths. Before addressing the spiritual direction relationship more directly in future chapters, I would like to address this larger context of soul nurture.

Spiritual Paths •

Across major faith traditions, Christian and non-Christian, we see a range of different paths upon which people live out their spiritual lives. The consistency of these paths across traditions reveals how much human beings share the same range of spiritual inclinations. Here is one way of looking at these paths in a simple summary form.[1]

1. The *devotional path* is marked by a very personal, intimate sense of divine reality. An affective relationship predominates. God is loving Father, Mother, Bridegroom, Lover. Prayer on this path gives special weight to praise, adoration, and thanksgiving. In some settings charismatic tongue speaking and healing may be encouraged. Beauty in God's creation may be greatly appreciated; this may involve being particularly drawn to the arts and nature. On this path we give ourselves to God as the Beloved, overflowing that love to those around us.

At its best this path opens and channels our deep spiritual yearning toward the Loved One beyond us, evoking self-forgetful appreciation and a strong, intimate, loving participation in life, transmuting negative emotions in ourselves and others. At its worst the devotional path can become sentimental, self-deceptive, privatistic, and cloudy, evading hard truths and actions in life. Also, it can seek and focus on feelings toward God that mistake the gifts of the Creator for full communion with the Creator.

2. The *path of action* emphasizes moral concerns: the "good" of ourselves, our neighbors, society, and nonhuman nature. God is redeeming judge and envisioner of a community of shalom, calling us to personal virtue, repentance, mutual correction, covenant faithfulness, social justice, community building, peace, and stewardship of the earth. Our vocation includes prophetic calls for justice, personal moral teaching, and sustained, sacrificial action on behalf of the common good. On this path we give ourselves to God through our neighbor, whose need mediates God's presence and calling for us.

At its best this path channels our spiritual yearning into self-forgetful, risk-taking, community-building, justice-seeking, neighbor-loving human concern and action for God's shalom in the world. At its worst it can engender self-righteous, closed-minded polarization rather than open, collaborative understanding in the truthful pursuit of human moral goals.

3. The *path of knowledge* centers on wisdom. God is the wise, knowing, seeing One; the image of God in us is revealed especially in conscious cultivation of spiritual knowledge. One emphasis on this path is analytical knowledge: what we can grasp cognitively, conceptually with our minds of "the really Real." We give ourselves to God through reason. Theology, philosophy, and the sciences discipline such thinking. A different emphasis moves toward intuitive knowledge, unmediated by the intellect. We give ourselves to God through intuitive awareness, with the help of particular meditation practices.

At its best the way of reason channels our spiritual yearning into a careful search for insights that help us critically understand, share with others, and inspire deep thinking and perspective concerning spiritual reality. At its worst this way confuses the insight with the spiritual reality it is interpreting.

The way of intuitive awareness at its best channels spiritual yearning into a quality of "direct seeing." Such sight allows a quality of firsthand awareness that can bring spiritual wisdom to a given subject or situation. At its worst this path can mistake intuition conditioned by subtle ego desires and fears for direct, innocent contact with the Holy.

4. Finally, we might identify a path that is not usually understood as such, the *path of fighting it all the way.* This is the path of greatest iconoclasm—idol-smashing. Every word about the Holy is suspected of masking some wishful fantasy. We would rather be spiritually sterile than false. We approach the holy kicking, screaming, and dragging our feet all the way. In effect, we give ourselves to God

through doubting anything that communicates false security rather than truth.

At its best this skeptical path lives out the first commandment: "You shall love no gods except me," guarding the great mystery of the Holy One's innermost name, "I am who I am" (Exod 3:14). This path can lead to a clearing of the false gods along the way and eventually, without conscious intention but with the hidden action of the Spirit, reveal the obscure radiance of the Real One. At its worst this pathless path can turn its followers toward cynicism, bitterness, or fear. Openness is lost. The disguised energy of spiritual yearning reveals itself only as a vague emptiness channeled perhaps into sensual drive and work, or lapsing into indolence. A blind, accidental universe is seen as final.

All of these paths belong to the human spiritual potential in each of us. They are not mutually exclusive. They are complementary. The human community needs all of them. Each path can be used to hide from divine truth or to freeze its dynamic quality. Each is corrected and given perspective by the others. Each can be a "way home." Probably we walk along each at some point in our lives. For some, there may be flashes of each one daily. For most of us, I think, one path will be dominant in our lives at any one time. Given the fact of increasing longevity in many countries, in the future we may see the possibility of more experience with all of these paths in the same person.

I don't think that any particular path is intrinsically superior to another, but one may be more called for at a given time in our lives. All of them can be underlain by a contemplative orientation that seeks to be present to God in the moment through all that shows itself. A spiritual director can sit appreciatively with someone as they affirm and test the path they are walking or seek to discern any called-for movement to another path.

Spiritual Practices •

There is no exclusive set of spiritual practices[2] for each spiritual path. Many particular practices crisscross all paths. Within a given path some of them may take on a particular coloration and emphasis, but these differences exist within a broadly shared range of possible basic practices.

Before speaking of particular practices let me raise up some potential pitfalls of spiritual practices in general, as well as their fundamental spiritual purposes as I understand them.

1. The first pitfall is the way practices can lead us to think that spiritual nurture is in our own hands. If we do so and so, then we will be spiritually rewarded. If we want to close the seeming gap between ourselves and God, this practice will do it. I can will my way to the possession of the kindom of God.

Behind such a view I think is a sense of an ultimately separate self that is able to enlarge itself to include the divine. This is a natural extension of those cultural values that assume that our ego selves are meant to be the central collection points for all kinds of goods in this world. The more we have, the more fulfilled, "filled," we will be. Spiritual goods are just another kind of goods in this view. So we become spiritual materialists, collecting all the practices we can as a way of filling up our starving spiritual stomachs.

Such a description puts crudely what has many subtle and unconscious forms. I know I am not immune to some of them. The problem with this view is that it can't work. It's based on an incorrect premise. The mature witnesses of deep Christian spiritual tradition again and again show us that spiritual nurture is not in our hands. It comes rather from the Wind of the Spirit, which "blows where it chooses, and you hear the sound of it, but you do not know where it comes from or where it is going. That is how it is with all who are born of the Spirit" (John 3:7–8).

Thus we are dealing with an uncontrollable, mysterious Wind blowing through life. We cannot domesticate it through a neat system of guidance and predicted progress. The Spirit breaks out of every cage we construct for it. In time, with the spiritual elders of the tradition, we come to see that it is for us to do the opposite of trying to control and collect things spiritually. Rather, it is for us to dispose ourselves to this holy Wind with an unconditional trust.

In time we are shown that we are made of that Spirit's energy. It lives in the seeds of our desires, thoughts, feelings, will, and body, if not necessarily in how these are manifest. Spiritual practice then is not about finding God somewhere else. It's about realizing the divine Presence in and around us all the time, praying for the empowerment to freely embrace that Presence as the very heart of our true soul-identity, and living out of its movements.

2. A second major pitfall in undertaking spiritual practice is an often subtle desire to have our cake and eat it too. We aspire toward spiritual practice, but we don't want to change. Our confused interior-ego friend wants to keep all the forms of safety, identity, and predictability that seem to have protected us. We want to go through the practice mainly as a protective ritual, one that we hope can keep or get everything the way our confused ego-identity wants things to be.

But this orientation engenders, I think, what Jesus exposed at various times as fearful, self-seeking kinds of practice that don't draw us to the kindom of God but try to preserve the soul-shrinking kindom of little self. In authentic spiritual practice I think our first prayer needs to be for the trust to release whatever we hold onto that keeps us separate from the One who truly lives at the heart of our lives. Spiritual practice gives us the opportunity to expose and embrace more and more fully the deep yearning in us for what is beyond the grasp of our mind. We can identify with the same yearning fire we encounter in all deep spiritual seekers, the fire that deep spiritual tradition interprets as God's fire in us. This fire would burn up the chaff of our lives and turn our consciousness and wills into transparencies of enlightened love that projects the divine image through us.

Do we want all our little desires to orbit around this deepest Desire? Are we willing to let whatever doesn't belong to divine freedom, love, and truth in us be purged as the Spirit sees we are ready, even if it leaves us disoriented and changed in ways we cannot predict? Do we want our deep soul to be nourished even if it empties us of everything with which we have identified as ultimately, rather than just relatively, who we are and what we need?

Such questions point to the radical nature of authentic spiritual practice. The practices themselves I think are largely neutral. They can be used to escape or to embrace life in God. It is not difficult to evade God in the name of God, as Jesus showed us in talking about empty ritual display in spiritual practice. I think it is the kind of conscious and unconscious desire that we bring to our practice that can go a long way in shaping our willingness to appreciate the Presence ever vibrant in our midst.

Of course, the Wind of the Spirit, being free, can surprise us in endless ways and raise up a spiritual temple in us from the fragments of whatever stones we bring. That freedom of the Spirit is very frustrating to the part of us that wants a well-ordered spiritual path from here to there—that wants our practices to get us somewhere. The same freedom of the Spirit gives us great hope, though, in the face of our sense of fumbling inadequacy and confusion on the spiritual path. Sometimes when there is a big crack in our spiritual self-confidence the Spirit is given space to draw us to deeper awareness on its own liberating terms.

Sharing across Faith Lines •

With this background as a base, let me select for comment some of the more specific, historic means of soul nurture that are available to us. We live in a time of increasing sharing across denominational and interfaith lines in terms of practice. There is far more openness among Protestants to take seriously practices that were often abandoned after the Reformation, just as there is far more study and prayer with scripture among Roman Catholics than there was before the Second Vatican Council. Classical icons, so intrinsic to Eastern Orthodox tradition, as well as the Jesus Prayer, have found their way into the prayer of many non-Orthodox Christians. Meditation practices have been shared and sometimes blended across major faith traditions. Hatha yoga, involving bodily postures and movements, has brought the body into spiritual practice in a fuller way.

In this sharing we see a growing willingness to claim the larger Christian heritage of practice across all mainstream Christian lines. Many people have gone beyond this to incorporate practices that have originated outside of intentional Christian practice but which have been found compatible with it. As I will say later in this book, I believe what makes a practice Christian is not its form but its intent. If our intent is to share more deeply the mind and heart of Christ, then that is what will guide its use.

The Scriptural Ground •

In looking at historic Christian practices, we can see most of their seeds in scripture. In the Gospels we find three fundamental practices held up: prayer, fasting, and almsgiving. *Almsgiving* can symbolize all the active forms of caring for life, individually and collectively, that are given to us during our lives, including stewardship of all our mental and physical possessions. *Fasting* can symbolize all those ways we sacrifice our lesser appetites for the greater one of hunger for the realization of union with God and for the fullness of God's shalom on earth. *Prayer* can symbolize all those individual and corporate ways we directly open ourselves, through all dimensions of our being and doing, to the One who we trust actively lives and guides through all that is. It is the practice of prayer in this sense that is the primary focus of this chapter.

Individual Prayer Practices •

Two primary avenues for individual practice present themselves. The first is *intentional concentrated practice* that happens in a special block of time during the day or week. The second avenue is *practicing the Presence through the day.* In both of these venues prayerful openness can take a receptive form that places us within a simple listening openness to the Presence. Prayer can also take a more active form, by which words, images, feelings, and gestures rise up in us, seeking to join God's prayer for us and the world. We or directees may uses terms like *contemplation* and *meditation* in describing different kinds of prayer, but these words do not carry consistent meanings in historic and current usage. As a result, it is more helpful to ask directees to describe the intent and actual process of their prayer rather than depending on potentially misleading labels like contemplation and meditation, unless you're very clear about what the person means by these words.

1. Intentional Concentrated Practice

What is done in a concentrated period of time will vary according to the individual's calling. What I find to be most important is that it be a practice that will help a person claim his or her desire for life in God and that the practice be aimed at opening the individual's whole life as it is to God as God is. The time can be anywhere from five minutes once a day to an hour or so twice or more times in a day. It's important that the amount of time given be realistic so that it can actually happen and, ideally, that it take place at the same time each day as a way of settling it into one's schedule without having to make a new decision about it each time.

The place where one takes this time can enhance one's freedom to be present. We need to decide what kind of a place would be best for us. For most people I think that such a place should be quiet, undisturbed, familiar, and enhanced with things to see that draw us to the Presence. These might include a candle, Bible, cross, flowers, or an icon, if the place is inside. If the space is outside, it might be by a body of water, a special tree, or some other inviting setting.

The content can include such elements as scripture, other spiritual reading, silent openness with or without a prayer form, intercession, petition, thanksgiving, confession, praise, sacred gestures and bodily movements, journal keeping, and music and other art media. For most people I think that the simpler the ingredients, the better, so that a certain spacious unhurriedness can mark the time. In the morning there could be some kind of dedication of the day to God. In the evening there might be some reflection on the day, asking God to show us where grace has shown itself that day. The same basic forms of prayer content can mark these times each day. They may spontaneously shift at times, if some other form shows itself as better able to carry the person's heart. In terms of particular prayer forms, I have spelled out many possibilities in an earlier book, *Living in the Presence* (Harper San Francisco, 1995).

The prayer time may extend itself into a number of hours on a day off, or longer on a private retreat. As I have written in great detail elsewhere,[3] it is particularly valuable to build in an extended period of receptive prayer time away from work, on a weekly basis whenever possible, a time that honors the historic rhythm of sabbath and ministry time. Sabbath time is an opportunity simply to appreciate life as it is in God without having to do anything else. It's a time to *be* in love and not *do* for love; a time to enjoy the creation and to rest. This will take different forms for different people. Sometimes it will be taken with other people. We need to notice what it is in terms of place and content that will most allow us to truly let go of our work and just enjoy life in God as an end in itself. Such an intrinsic communing with God is part of our calling, one that complements our calling to care for the world with our particular gifts. That second calling at its best flows out of our sense of intrinsic communion with God. Our work then is not only *our* work. It is, at least in our intent, *God*'s work with and through our work. (I will return to this subject in chapter seven, in the section, "Workplace Spirituality.")

JOURNAL KEEPING

Let me say a little more in detail about journal keeping, since this is such a widespread and helpful practice for many people and a spiritual director may well be asked about it. Reflection on the spiritual journey can give us a sense of grace operating in our lives in ways that not only may help us understand its patterns but also help us to relax our grasping for security. If we sense grace present, even if it is in a surprising or unwanted form, we can trust a little more that transcendent caring is happening. We don't have to try and force this caring; rather, we should just be attentive to and cooperative with the caring that shows itself. We don't have to defend ourselves against a sense of ultimately hostile or blind forces. There are relatively hostile forces that require vigilance. However, deep Christian tradition points to trusting, not primarily in our own isolated prowess or in the ultimacy of these blind or hostile forces, but in a collaborative flow of the powers of Light in and around us.

Journal keeping, as it helps us to be in touch with this hidden flow of grace in our lives, can include any form of imaging: poetry, prose, dialogue, pictorial imagining. These can be either spontaneous, or focused on some particular situation or theme. They can deal with thoughts, feelings, intuitions, events, and dreams,[4] and with the past, present, and future.

The more casual our journaling, the better. If it is too "heavy," too full of expected "good" insight, ego easily becomes involved in it. No longer is something flowing freely through us, but we are trying to force something or trying to look good. There is an extreme form of avoiding this tendency in a Zen writing practice, wherein no possessive pronoun is allowed to be used. For example, the sentence, "hand moves across page with many words," can leave more of a sense of non-ego-focused open presence than, "I am writing down a lot of my thoughts in my journal."

Frequency of entry in a journal is a very individual matter. As a rule of thumb, if we are just beginning, then a more disciplined practice of daily entry might be desirable during the first few months, as a way of establishing the habit. Later it can be more sporadic. The amount of time taken is also a very individual matter. It may be for a minute; it may be for an hour.

Since we need to be free to write openly, we may have written what is not meant for public knowledge. To help insure privacy we can invent certain key code words that disguise what we are saying to all but ourselves. Another possibility is to periodically burn the journal, which may have the additional value of helping us let go of a past to which we have become attached, and freer for the fresh grace of a new time.

Sometimes it might be helpful to read over the patterns in the journal dating back for a period of weeks or months. In this way we may sense any addictions that need healing and the grace that is healing—and calling. We may sense a shift in our vocation in some way, along with the grace to respond. Suggesting that directees pray over any recent journal entries before coming to a direction session and that they consider looking at their journals as the scripture of their lives can provide an incentive for spiritual journaling and possible content for the direction session. However, another approach is to suggest that directees sometimes make entries simply as a way of letting things go to God, with no intention of returning to read them.

For some people journal keeping is a practice that, once tried, just does not show itself to be a needed practice. For others, too much time and attention are given to it, which can tempt them to overfascination and overconcern with themselves. There may be particularly important periods when much writing time is called for. However, if it takes up too many hours, I think journal keeping can lose the general lightness that needs to be present in all spiritual disciplines, lest we find ourselves subtly turning them into ways that try to force grace and clarity beyond what is possible, rather than simply appreciating the mysterious, evolving grace that is.

In this and every discipline it is crucial to realize that we cannot make happen or understand what we are not ready for. Every practice involves attentive patience, a way of receptively inviting what needs to happen that only God knows, a way of reinforcing trust in an incipient wholeness in God that unfolds as it unfolds. Every practice, then, potentially frees us to be a little more attentive to the loving, joyful/painful truths given in our lives and less obedient to fantasies that we in our wounded nature would substitute.[5]

RULE OF LIFE

The monastic traditions of certain faith bodies live by a corporate rule of life. Historically, simplified versions of these rules have often been established for lay associates of these communities. That practice has widened beyond lay associates to the development of individually adapted rules of life for those who want to commit to a particular structure for the nurture of their souls. Such a rule can include many elements of practice that I have already mentioned, as well as others. Traditionally they include such things as set-apart prayer times with daily lectionary-based scriptural readings, Sunday Eucharist, intercession, simplicity in living, charitable giving, the rite of reconciliation, the use of one's gifts for particular called-for kinds of care and creativity in God's world, extended times for retreat, and seeing a spiritual director regularly. Over time, some of these practices have been incorporated into the expected spiritual discipline of clergy.

Some people find that committing themselves to such a rule provides them with the extra incentive they need to steadily carry out a serious spiritual practice in the face of dominant cultural and family values and rhythms that don't support their serious spiritual calling. The spiritual director may be called upon to help a directee to discern the kind of rule that is called for and to aid in evaluating its fruits and form from time to time. As mentioned earlier regarding daily practice, such a rule needs to be realistic in terms of what a person feels able and called to sustain. It should not be taken on as a rigid straightjacket that must be worn at all costs, but rather as a sign of one's desire for a serious spiritual life incarnated through particular practices, which at times may not hold up in the face of life's exigencies. The person is not owned by the rule, but by the desire for God being lived out through it wherever possible.

2. Practicing the Presence through the Day

The second avenue for individual practice is comprised of the intent and practice we weave into the day, excluding specially set-apart times. This is practicing the Presence of God through the events, feelings, thoughts, and actions of our daily lives. In chapter seven I mention some particular possibilities related to the workplace and other arenas. Here let me just emphasize the fundamental trusting attitude of appreciating the Spirit living through and around us as we move through the day's happenings. We do not have to bring God into the day. God's energy is at the core of everything that is. Rather, we need to pray for a trusting recognition of this underlying guiding Presence and to open our desire to live out of that Presence in all situations of the day as best we can.

When you notice that you are feeling separated from the Presence, you might want to take a deep, slow breath and ask that you be able to remember the Presence that connects you to all that is true, free, and needed in this moment. This isn't always possible. Sometimes we are trapped in our unfreedoms and separations, and we just have to rest content with *wanting* to want God now. We might want to include in our prayer at the beginning of the day a plea that we be helped to remember God's Presence enveloping our presence throughout the day. This doesn't have to be a hard, separate act of remembering; it can be a simple, light allowing of the Presence to appear in our consciousness, or at least in our *desire* for that appearance, freeing the moment for what it is meant to be as much as possible.

Directees' ways of concentrated prayer practice and of being present for God during the day's activities may well find their way into a spiritual direction session. Directees might speak of what grace and guidance are being shown them through such times. They also may need to talk about how they are feeling called to change their practices in ways that are more life-giving. Over time, many practices may fall away as people find themselves living more and more directly and spontaneously out of the present moment in God.

Active, mentally busy practices especially may fall away for more contemplatively called people. John of the Cross said from his experience that we can reach a point when we simply cannot pray in an active way and yet we deeply desire God at the center of our being. A person's prayer may then become more of a receptive, structureless, contentless, open presence. John writes that the spiritual director needs to be very supportive of a person if this point is reached, and not try to press the directee back into active prayer.[6]

Gathering in Small Groups for Different Kinds of Prayerful Presence •

At the core of Jesus' ministerial life we see him meeting again and again with a small group of disciples, whom he later called friends. Today there has been a great resurgence of small groups in churches and other spiritual centers, where people gather together to open their souls in prayer. These can take place in weekly groups or in quiet days or retreat settings. They can take all kinds of forms. Some focus on the teaching and practice of one particular form of contemplative prayer, such as centering prayer, and include much communal silence. Others read scripture with the intent of listening for the Spirit's voice through it, as in classical *lectio divina,* where one moves through steps from listening and digesting attentively to prayer and open contemplative presence. Others gather for discernment, listening for corporate or individual guidance related to particular potential callings of the Spirit. Still others gather for praise and song, for confession and forgiveness, for Eucharist and other sacramental rites, and for laying on of hands for healing. Some combine a number of these purposes in an ongoing group.

People gathered with a shared hunger for God bring together a quality of energy that can be enormously supportive. At the Shalem Institute, for example, we have many such groups, especially ones that share guided listening prayer and reflection together. Over the years I have heard countless people tell me how important these gatherings have been for them. In the purest shared presence together many people find that their normal securing, highly boundaried sense of self begins to dissolve and their sense of God as a boundaried object lessens as well. They are left beyond subject-object definitions in open presence, identified with the sacred blazing or smoldering fire or open spaciousness at the heart of their being. Here they sometimes speak of being given a sense of their true Home. They also speak of their fears and unreadiness that they feel keep them circling rather than entering a holy place of full openness.

When people gather together with others expressing the same yearnings and frustrations that they have experienced, it helps to make this deep place of spiritual practice an opportunity for honest and supportive listening. It also reinforces their sense of the reality rather than the illusion of the spiritual yearning for the "more" of God that often haunts them. They are encouraged by the group's presence not to be put off by their own fears and frustrations and to return again and again to the group, claiming their birthright as intimate offspring of the great Wellspring. Most of these people have an individual contemplative practice away from the group and sometimes stop meeting with a group. I have seen many of them return years later for a retreat or a group experience when they feel drawn to open further their deep nature and calling in God.

Other Kinds of Groupings •

I will be giving attention to group spiritual direction in chapter five and to the gathering for corporate worship/ liturgy in chapter seven. Here I will just mention what a spiritually formative place corporate worship is for many people. It is the baseline of historic gathering to listen and pray collectively. However, many people have had bad as well as good experiences during such gatherings. These gatherings can be very blessed, or they can have ways of distorting and hiding the Gospel that can make participation very painful. Such experiences may well be brought to the spiritual director to be opened for healing and discernment of the person's call at this point in terms of corporate worship.

Study groups, whether in preparation for church membership, or for biblical, theological, or spiritual book reflection, are widespread. Today I sense that they are more often including serious prayer time as well as study, so that they more fully blend head and heart and become a little more of a spiritual formation group. Some people find their way to God through their minds, and some of the revelations that come to them through such groups can also surface in a spiritual direction session. The direction session is not meant to be a study session, however, and the director needs to draw the person's excitement or frustration with a given insight to the person's sense of spiritual reality, calling, and prayer.

The spiritual nurture that we find in gatherings of our families and other communal circles of our lives will be addressed in chapter seven.

Other Communal Resources •

Many churches provide a broad kind of spiritual nurture by means of liturgical frameworks that take members together through seasons of the church year. These can provide a rhythm of self-examination, fasting, feasting, celebration, and reliving the deep mysteries of the Christian experience in scripture. They can provide a shared transcendent focus that aids our resistance of the temptation to fragment and focus on petty things as a community. Sometimes the seasons seem artificial and don't fit our personal spiritual situation very well, yet they always remind us of the universal scheme of things and catch us up in a larger spiritual rhythm than our own.

Churches often include a calendar of saints who are honored at particular times through the year. This exposure gives opportunity for a range of spiritual heroes to be held before us as signs of grace and ways into the Holy. I think it is sad that in Roman Catholic and Orthodox traditions more of these saints are not lay and married people; this makes it difficult for many of us to identify with the saints' and to view these states of life as paths to the *spiritual*. It's also sad that so many of the saints' biographies are often undocumented or overly idealized. Even so, I think they can provide the guidance of a living chain of risk-taking and blessed spiritual seekers that is infinitely more inspiring and instructive to the average person than abstract theological ideas cut off from their human incarnations.

In today's churches we often find a variety of spiritually deep people held up for inspiration who are not part of a tradition's list of certified holy people. That actually is an ancient Church tradition. The "official" saints are simply those few who have lasted in people's memories and inspiration over time and become officially recognized as people who have special value for the inspiration of the whole church. The "unofficial" saints form a far more extensive list. The reputation of these saints are complemented by the influence of the large numbers of holy people experienced alive in churches and society today. A directee may well have been spiritually inspired in a special way by some particular living person. Such living saints have a way of incarnating and communicating spiritual truth in a very personal way, as did the desert mothers and fathers with those who were close to them.

The Spiral of the Spiritual Life •

So much of the spiritual life, I think, is lived in a spiral of touching into the divine Fire and circling away again, then coming back at a deeper level, often very different than we would have predicted it to be. A group of people with whom we share direct presence and a desire for God (as well as the indirect group of living and past saints with whom we also share a kind of spiritual community) can be a very precious environment for nurturing the soul. As we found out many years ago at Shalem, however, an intentional group does not allow enough time for the kind of personal spiritual sharing that some people need at a given point in their lives. What has happened to them in the group and in the other areas of their lives leads them to crave more time to reflect on what is developing and what is called for on their spiritual journey. As previously mentioned, such a desire has also been stimulated in individuals through their participation in one or more of many popular spiritual movements. The stimulus of these group experiences leaves some people disoriented and reoriented in ways that cry out for more attention to what the Spirit is up to within them. The spiritual director can become a steady, prayerful presence through all that is happening.

CHAPTER 5

HOW DO WE RECOGNIZE A SPIRITUAL COMPANION?

If we want to know the qualities of an authentic spiritual companion, I think it's best to begin with our own experience. If we look over our own times with people who we felt really assisted our presence for God in a way that gave us deep room to notice the hidden currents of the Spirit in our lives, we could come up with a list of qualities that would tell us a lot about what has been important to us. These qualities would likely vary among us in terms of emphasis, but they would likely overlap a great deal.

If we have been drawn to a particular person many times to listen with us for the Spirit's ways in our lives, then we have known someone who likely reflects the fundamental historic calling of a spiritual companion, someone with a true charism for this ministry. The marks of this charism historically are these:

1. People come to such spiritual companions spontaneously and repeatedly to speak of their yearnings and life in God.

2. The companion cares about these people at the fundamentally spiritual level of their lives and feels called to be with and pray for them.

3. The companion desires and humbly pursues union and life in God through all things.

I will speak about some other qualities that are important in a spiritual companion, but these three I believe form the historic foundation.

Further Important Qualities of the Companion •

In the Gospels Jesus implies qualities of humble service, love, empowered relation to himself, to God, to the indwelling, discerning Spirit, and to the community of faith. Given the many weaknesses of the disciples, he certainly did not imply moral and spiritual perfection as necessary qualifications. A willingness for repentance and a trust in and sharing of ongoing divine forgiveness and new life flowing from a very intimate God were what counted most.

St. Paul spells out the fruit of the Spirit, previously mentioned, that by implication should mark a spiritual companion: love, joy, peace, patience, kindness, generosity, faithfulness, gentleness, and self-control (Gal 5:22). Paul also speaks of pleasing God and not people when we speak (1 Thess 2:4). He further speaks of attending our whole being, spirit, soul, and body (1 Thess 5:23).

As we read scripture, we can be alert to other implied qualities that strike us.

For the desert fathers and mothers, a steady personal qualification held up for a spiritual guide was compunction: a sign of valid repentance, *metanoia*, conversion, "a sense of the truth of meeting the infinitely real in the center of one's nothingness,"[1] and the fruit of tranquility *(hesychia),* purity of heart.

John of the Cross adds a qualification that varies with the relationship. Directors should be able not merely to aim at guiding souls according to their own way, but should determine if they (directors) can see the way "by which God is leading the soul, and if they know it not, let them leave the soul in peace and not disturb it."[2] John is expressing concern about directors who try to impose their own way on directees, without paying attention to the distinctive ways in which God is guiding their lives.

Teresa of Avila saw the importance of good judgment and experience in the director. If the director has learning (especially in scripture), so much the better, but people with learning can be sought out separately. She also valued kindness (i.e., the director is interested, trusting, consoling).[3]

Francis de Sales, in the seventeenth century, added that the director should be a faithful friend who is able to help a person follow and not outrun grace.[4]

More recent commentators have added such qualities as simplicity (in the sense of not being focused on your own self-discovery and importance); the humility to learn with and through the directee; the willingness to hold confidences; the capacity to be an awakener of what is already there; the ability to balance strength and gentleness, mental clarity, intuitiveness, and objectivity and receptivity.[5] Thomas Merton speaks of the director as someone willing to see that their first duty is "To see to his own interior life and take time for prayer and meditation, since you never will be able to give to others what you do not possess yourself."[6]

This last comment reflects an undercurrent in Christian spiritual tradition. Spiritual guidance is not primarily a matter of using one's accumulated skills, but rather of facing into the call to let ourselves be stripped of illusion and sin in the face of the great Love, which frees us to be ever more transparent and truly present with someone. Our own experience in touching and glancing away from the same divine reality with which our directee struggles gives us a common bond and sympathetic perception. However, in one sense I think the last part of Merton's quote could give a distorted view of direction. I believe it is finally God's grace that does the "giving" in the relationship, not the director. The director may at times be a vessel of that grace, but the particular grace may be something that the director her/himself does *not* possess. Part of the wonder of grace is the way it is free to come to us through limited vessels who may never themselves have received grace in that form.

Contemplative Presence •

The list of qualities above can be very intimidating for a director. I don't believe that any of us can consistently manifest them. They are grounds for great humility and awe in approaching the mystery of another soul with our own soul and the Spirit's presence. They leave us dependent on the mercy of God, as we trust that the Spirit can flow between us just as we are. From a contemplative standpoint, what is most important is not the knowledge and strengths we bring so much as our willingness to be very simply present to God for the directee, with a mind of "unknowing," spacious and available for we don't know what, yet trusting God to show us whatever we need to see.

Such a contemplatively oriented director need not try to do anything more. Their simple, trusting-of-God, leaning-back-into-God presence provides a spaciousness for directees that invites them deeper than their ego-coping surface, down to where their deep soul has an opportunity to show its yearning for God and appreciation of the divine currents running through their lives.

The director need not verbally speak during the entire session, and yet their soul-presence does speak, on a deeper level. When that depth is shared together with the directee, their souls and the Spirit are in communication in both hidden and sometimes visible ways. They touch into their shared dynamic nature in God. Such deep sharing may exist for only a very brief time together, but it can make up for longer periods of disconnection that may be apparent during the session. The directee and/or the director are shown something of their being that is often covered over by the hype of daily living. For a moment, at least, they know what it is to have and to be a real soul-friend.

We can't "make" such times happen. A direction session may be full of mundane words back and forth that seem to remain more on the surface of things. And yet even these times can surprise us in the fruit they sometimes bear. The Spirit can show up in the mundane details. So directors can approach a session without expectation of anything in particular happening, and yet with an expectation that the Holy Spirit is hidden in the seeds of all the words, feelings, actions, and silences that show themselves. Thus the Spirit will draw the directee toward realization of union and divine compassion, and will draw the director as well.

Different Forms of Spiritual Companionship Today •

It might help us to recognize the kind of spiritual companionship we need and are meant to offer by understanding the choices that are available. The growth of

spiritual companionship in our time has led to a sometimes confusing array of ways such companionship is
understood and offered. Some of these ways go back deep
in the tradition; others have been born much more
recently. Here is an outline of some types of companionship. They are not necessarily mutually exclusive. Authentic spiritual companionship can happen in any of these
forms. Each of us has to decide which form will most fully
allow our awareness and freedom for God.[7]

1. Master/Disciple Relationship. This is the oldest form
of spiritual companioning. We see it with the desert
fathers and mothers and still in many of the monastic traditions, especially Eastern Orthodox, that grew from
those desert beginnings. We see it frequently in Eastern
religious traditions as well. The master is seen as a realized being who can mirror for us the depths of our condition and soul. In time the disciple may share the master's
realization of divine truth and in turn become a master
for others. The disciple's realization is often seen to
include the need to give up a separate ego-will through
obedience to the master.

A strength of this tradition is the intense, energetic
commitment that it engenders in the disciple, a willingness to let go of everything for the sake of realization
through the path laid out by the master. A difficulty with
this kind of relationship is the fact that unenlightened
parts of the master's mind can go unrecognized, possibly
causing exploitation of the disciple. This could potentially lead, in time, to the disciple's spiritual, mental, or
physical harm and disillusionment.

2. Gifted Spiritual Direction. This involves a regular
relationship with a director who meets the historic criteria for the charism of this ministry mentioned at the

beginning of this chapter. The director may have no formal training, but whether they do or not, others seek them out and they feel called to respond. The locus of discernment may vary. Until the middle of the twentieth century I would expect that it rested more with the director and, since that time, as many churches and modern culture in general have become more democratized, the locus has steadily shifted toward the directee. Sometimes these directors will meet with other directors in the kind of peer group described in the next chapter.

This form of direction represents a large number of contemporary directors. Its strength lies in the way it reflects the historic marks of a spiritual director, its prayerful attention to the soul of the directee, and its relatively wide and often free availability. An occasional limitation sometimes results when the director, probably due to a lack of spiritual confidence, suppresses even a gentle challenge to the directee that has come to them and might truly be of the Spirit. This is the basic kind of spiritual direction relationship that will be held up and described in this book.

3. Counseling-Inspired Spiritual Direction. This form of relationship takes some of its cues from one or more of the many therapeutic forms of counseling that are so widespread in North America and growing elsewhere. The kind of relationship that I think most often emerges from these influences tends to be a more formal kind of relationship in which the director is seen as expert helper who is caring but needs a certain professional distance from the directee for effectiveness. The director has received certification training that often includes some psychologically influenced understandings and analytical techniques, along with formal learning in the field of historic spiritual life and direction. These directors are often in some supervisory relationship with others and are more likely to charge for their time than those directors in the last category. The locus of final discernment, whether with the director or directee, would vary, depending upon the particular director's values.

This form of direction, I believe, also represents a large number of contemporary directors. One of its potential strengths is the seriousness with which preparation and accountability are regarded. One of its potential weaknesses is the possibility that the directee might be subtly influenced to turn away from a simple, open presence to God and to become more dependent on the director's conditioned knowledge and images. That is, instead of this knowledge helpfully surrounding a simple, "unknowing," given-to-God quality of presence, it would completely take over the director's consciousness, losing a sense of immediate givenness to the "third party" in the relationship: the Holy Spirit.

4. Eldering and Discipling. These are terms often used in evangelically oriented churches to refer to ministries that assist members of these faith communities. Both of these ministerial approaches may involve a central focus on scripturally grounded moral and other formational guidance, with the discernment process more predominantly in the hands of the elder, as opposed to listening openly together for how the Spirit is moving within the person. As historical spiritual direction has become more widely known in these communities, I have sensed that this is shifting some Evangelicals' way of being present in such a relationship.

I don't feel qualified to speak about the strengths and limitations of these Evangelical traditions. Even with my limited understanding, I see strength in the great seriousness with which a relationship with Christ, scripture, and a whole religious way of life is pursued. I would suspect that a weakness might be the lack of room given for deep listening to the mysterious and often surprising ways that the Spirit moves within a person's life.

5. Informal Relationships. In addition to the more regular, intentional relationships normally involved in those forms of direction mentioned thus far, there are many kinds of informal spiritual relationships. We may well have one or more of these in addition to or in place of the more formal ones. Many of us have had wisdom figures among our family or friends with whom we occasionally share some dimension of our spiritual life. Occasionally we may form a deep connectedness with someone with whom we feel a great overlap in our spiritual journeys. Then there are those one-time encounters—on a retreat, at church, or in some other setting—where we really touched into God with another person.

These relationships often involve a mutual sharing rather than one-way direction. They are spontaneous relationships that have no particular structure, but where there is a mutual desire to talk of God in their lives. One strength of such relationships is their gifted, unplanned quality, which allows sharing in a particularly free and uncontrived manner. In a relationship characterized by much give and take, one limitation might be a wandering focus, wherein one or both persons really need more centering time, with a steady concentration on what's happening in their spiritual lives.

6. Mutual Spiritual Direction Relationships. All direction is in some sense mutual. The director can be opened to particular grace during a session just as much as the directee. However, I think there is great value in allowing a primary focus on one person at a time for the sake of intensity and depth of focus. This may happen for some people in a give-and-take approach as well, but I think it is less likely. We can experiment with both models and find out for ourselves what is best for us.

A mutual relationship is possible while still maintaining a focus on one person at a time for a given hour. That is, one person can be the focus for an hour, and the other in the second hour or at a separate time. It may be, though, that a person to whom you are drawn as a spiritual companion is already in a direction relationship with someone else. Or the person may be right for you as a director, but you may not be right for her/him (or vice versa). Because of this I think that the "ideal fit" of two people for each other is fairly rare. I experienced such a relationship myself for many years and I can vouch for the blessing it can be. Frequently I have found that a strength of such a relationship is that when one person says something about his or her spiritual life, it can end up having great relevance to the other person's spiritual life as well. Being able to shift attention to the other person in a second hour gives opportunity for that avenue to be explored together. A potential weakness of such a relationship might be a slightly lessened sense of freedom for the person who is director in the first hour to fully listen to God for the other person or to feel fully free to challenge the other person if they feel moved to do so, because they are aware that they will be speaking about themselves in the second hour.

Group Spiritual Direction •

There is a growing interest in gathering together with a few other people for spiritual direction rather than with only one other person. This approach can incorporate different models of spiritual direction, but I will focus here on the well-tested one that Shalem Institute has used for many years. Out of that experience has come a book, *Group Spiritual Direction* (Paulist Press, 1997), by one of our staff, Rose Mary Dougherty, S.S.N.D., as well as a videotape with the same name (also available from Paulist Press).

As with one-on-one spiritual direction, people gather on a regular basis to listen for God in their lives. In a group there is less time for the sharing of one's own life, but echoes of what one needs to hear for oneself often come from listening to others' sharing of the way the Spirit seems to be moving in them. Everyone in the group becomes a spiritual director by listening and responding to the others in the group, just as everyone is a directee of all the others in the group.

In forming a new group it is important to have a group facilitator who is experienced with group direction, or at least who is experienced with one-to-one direction and has read about group direction. Such a person can model the process of group direction and intervene when a group seems to lose a climate of prayerful listening. The facilitator can also serve as convener and timekeeper for the group. For the sake of time this person normally would not be a directee in the group but would otherwise participate fully in its life.

In the successful process developed by Sister Rose Mary Dougherty at Shalem, three or four participants form a group. If more people are interested, different small groups can meet in separate rooms, joining together for about twenty minutes of prayer and silence before separating. A longer meeting on the first day can be helpful for developing an understanding of the group's process and its method of faith sharing. The first few meetings can be every two weeks, and after that the meetings can happen monthly, for ten months. The group can then take a two-month break (especially during the summer), after which individuals can decide whether or not they want to continue for another year.

The structure of the small group model successfully tested at Shalem is as follows:

1. Silence for five minutes, with an invitation for someone to begin sharing when she or he feels ready.

2. Sharing by one person for ten to fifteen minutes.

3. Silence for three to four minutes to help the group members become freer to respond from a place of prayer.

4. Response invited by the facilitator for ten minutes.

5. Silence for about five minutes, requesting prayer for the participants; the directee may use that time to take notes.

6. Repeat of the process, with a short break midway, until all members have presented.

7. Prayer for any absent members, which can be inserted anywhere in the meeting's process, reflecting intercession as the most important thing that members of the group can offer one another, both in the meeting and between meetings.

8. Reflection on the sense of prayerfulness within the group and within individuals for about ten minutes.

This provides the barest outline of a way of understanding and offering group spiritual direction. If you are potentially drawn to move in this direction, I would strongly urge your reading of Rose Mary Dougherty's book for an understanding of readiness for and development of such a group. My own sense is that group spiritual direction is just beginning to be understood as a viable option for many people, and that we will be seeing much more of it in the future.[8] If such a group is made up of people in a particular congregation, it could indirectly contribute to the spiritual deepening of the congregation in the ways group members over time may begin to approach worship, meetings, activities, and corporate decisions with a greater sense of listening for God and intercession. Such a contribution can also result from people in one-to-one direction, but in group direction there is the added impact of numbers and the practice of being in a meeting with other church members in an intimately prayerful and attentive way.

CHAPTER 6

HOW ARE WE PRESENT WITH ANOTHER AS SPIRITUAL COMPANION?

Spiritual direction has an oral tradition behind it. We learn what it's about by being involved in the process with a director. The person or persons who have been spiritual companions for us, however informal or sporadic those relationships were, have shown us much about what is important in being present to God for another person's soul. Sometimes our experience has been negative, and we have learned how *not* to be present with someone. We are not blind followers of our directors. We are unique individuals who bring our own strengths and limitations to a relationship. Our hope is that in our willingness to be open to God for the sake of our directee, the Spirit will show itself between us in fruitful ways, despite and even through our limitations. That willingness is the greatest gift we bring to the relationship.

Earlier I spoke of valuing an "unknowing" mind as spiritual director. If we truly want to be open directly to God in the session, we need to let ourselves drop behind all we think we know about the directee with our minds and rest in the simple openness of our spiritual hearts. We can bring to that openness our desire to join God's hope for this person, as well as our desire for that hope to show itself between us in ways we can't predict.

More precisely, we want to be open to whatever we may be shown about what the Spirit's wise loving in this person's soul is inviting now, and how the directee's receptive/resistant spirit is shaping a response in accordance with its own nature. We may have hints of this interior creative process from what the directee has said in the current and past sessions together. But it is a never-ending process of God's dynamic Love and the person's free, dynamic spirit subtly sparking together ever new life, communion, and calling.

Thus, what is happening within the directee is always stretching beyond what either director or directee knows from the past. We are pioneers together in uncharted spiritual waters, because no one has ever lived the life of this unique shaping of God's image who sits before us. We do have the stories of others who have articulated their spiritual journeys, and these are helpful in showing us something of what is possible in our walk in the Spirit. But every story is distinctive, so we can only be present in trust to what we don't know until the Spirit shows itself.

What we may be given to know then will only be the leading edge of what is an ongoing process. The directee is an emerging human design growing from the dance of his spirit and God's Spirit, and the design is never completed in this lifetime. As directors we are privileged to sit in on this process with the directees and offer our openness to God for their sake, hoping that our openness will serve their openness to the leading dance steps of the Spirit in their lives.

Since we're opening ourselves to the uncontrollable and vast/intimate mystery of divine Presence in our own and the other person's life in spiritual direction, we bring a sense of awe to the process. If we are used to feeling in charge of things and having a clear sense of where things are going, spiritual direction will be particularly challenging. It requires more trust and tolerance of ambiguity than clarity and control. At the opposite pole, if we are used to a lot of self-doubt about our ways of being present to people, then being a spiritual companion can also be challenging. We can feel completely inadequate, in the dark, and fearful of missing what we need to hear and when we need to speak— or not speak. A certain lack of confidence is actually good in a direction relationship, because it leaves us turning to God rather than turning to a sense of our own autonomous resources. If we have too little confidence, though, we are likely to become more focused on ourselves and our worry about "getting it right," taking us away from an interior focus on simple givenness to God in the moment.

On a more subconscious level I think we can also bring a fear of what might show itself to us. I know that I have felt a wave of resistance before entering a time with a spiritual companion, which I attribute to this fear of the unknown. That wave is usually countered by a sense of trust that God has only love in mind for us, be that tough or soft love. Whatever is revealed that shakes up my or my directee's security-seeking ways can be trusted to be life-giving in the end. Such empowered trust, beyond any anxiety about the time, is necessary for our willing openness during the session. When it is not present ahead of time in a directee, we might find this to be one reason behind their missing meetings, leaving the relationship, or remaining on a defensive and evasive-of-God level during the time of meeting.

Ingredients of the Meeting •

Because we often come to a spiritual direction time with both anticipation and fear, openness and closedness to our deep souls in God, it can be helpful to provide a structure for the time that invites as much openness as possible.

Physical Environment. If the Holy Spirit so wills, good spiritual direction can happen in the worst possible environment. But given the anxious heart, crowded mind, and bodily tension that can be brought to a direction session, an inviting physical environment might help to reduce these potential barriers to deep listening. If the place where you meet is "cluttered" with noise, interruptions of people (in person or on the phone), glaring lights, and a desk piled with debris between you and the person, these might reinforce a cluttered mind. Even the chair can be a problem. A badly contoured chair that gives either discomfort or too much comfort might prove distracting.

The simpler, quieter, and more aesthetically warm the room, the more your space might invite a simpler, quieter, more easeful presence. A simple, small chapel or prayer room could be helpful for some people, though some others might find them intimidating, associating them with a sense of inhibition they may feel in a church setting. A candle lit between you can symbolize the larger living Presence, the real Director of the session, whom you have both come together to hear, both of you listening for the directions of the Spirit. A simple object from nature, such as a flower, or a sacred symbol, perhaps an icon or a cross, might be inviting for some people.

Some people meet in their homes. This can be fine and is sometimes the only or best place available, but if young children are present it sometimes can prove disruptive (though of course the Spirit sometimes uses disruptions, like anything else!). If you're married and meeting in an empty house with someone of the opposite sex, some spouses can find such meetings threatening. In such cases it might be best to seek out a more public place to meet if that is possible, such as a room or office in a church. Some people meet in restaurants, but this can be a distracting and inhibiting environment. Once again, the Spirit can move in *any* environment as it wills, but we might *hear* those movements more easily in some environments than others.

Beginning the Session. Both director and directee can be helped to drop beneath the surface crowdedness and resistance to presence for God by allowing for some kind of prayerful spaciousness at the start of the time. This might include such things as a scripture passage and/or prayer, and if you or they seem particularly stressed or tired, a few long, slow breaths. Above all, though, I think this time can benefit from five minutes or so of silence, inviting the directee (and yourself) to immediately open whatever appears in the mind to God, or whatever other words of invitation you might be moved to give.

Such silent time can leave both you and the directee calmer and freer to listen from the deep soul rather than from ego-level fears and busyness. Spiritual direction involves a special kind of asceticism in the sense of being willing to drop behind that ego level of identity to our deeper, freer identity in the image of God. From that identity flows God's Spirit in our spirit, and the spontaneous words that come through us are more likely to show what we need to hear.

Silent times can be valuable at moments other than the beginning of the session. Both the directee and the director should feel free to call for a moment of silence whenever either senses that the dialogue has become too forced or irrelevant to the intent of spiritual direction. Another kind of silent time can be respected as well: those times when a profound sense of Presence or discernment has struck, and the directee just needs to let it sink in wordlessly. Reverencing such silent times helps us to remember that when a person is directly touched by the Spirit, words not only are not needed but could draw them away from the ineffable communion that is accomplishing what is needed wordlessly. The director is a silent, appreciative, prayerful human presence during such a time.

The Rest of the Session. The director invites the directee to share whatever they are moved to share about the way the Holy Spirit seems to have been moving in their life since the last meeting. Any aspect of life can be brought, not just their prayer life, since God's Spirit is alive in every dimension of living. It's important that the focus remain on probing what the Spirit seems to be up to in what is brought and how the directee is responding, rather than on human issues and problem solving in which one's desire for God has lost centrality. Since we are so often conditioned to a psychological way of looking at our lives, insulated from any sense of divine involvement, it can take real intentionality to maintain a focus on God's mysterious Presence.

Even though anything in one's life that seems to be showing something of divine Presence and invitation is an appropriate topic for a session, I think there is need at some point in most sessions to ask about what is happening in the person's intentional *prayer life,* the life of direct relationship with God's Spirit in Christ (I talked about forms of this life in chapter four). How is prayer happening? How is it the same or shifting, empty or full, talky or listening? What is spontaneously showing itself in these times that seems of the Spirit? How is the directee taking intentional times for prayer, and how are they trying to practice the Presence through daily activities? What desires do they bring to their prayer?

Intentional prayer can reveal a lot about the directee's desire for or fear of God, and how the Spirit seems to be whispering in his or her life. Such prayer, beyond whatever particular content or fruits it may have, at bottom can be seen as a way to claim our desire for a fuller realized union with God and God's love in and through our lives and the world's life. It's a way of exposing ourselves to God's desire for us and the world, and a way of asking for the empowerment of whatever way of being and doing is called for through us in this life. At its purest we can sense the Holy Spirit praying in us, so that our prayer is God's prayer in us reaching for God's life beyond us. Our being is a precious and unique carrier of that Presence. We are not ultimately separate from it.

A directee may have prepared for the session a bit through such means as looking over their journal entries for the past month and by asking in prayer to be shown what they need to see when they come to the meeting. Or the directee may come with no particular preparation, simply wanting to be open to God in the moment. Something may come to them in the initial silence that shows some glimmers of the Spirit moving in their lives. I think it's important to treat the session itself as a laboratory of the Spirit rather than a "time out" to reflect on what has been happening in the past. Whatever may be brought from the past is brought to this living moment of the eternal Presence, and that living Presence is given room to shape in us what is heard and said. Both director and directee can try to be open to the surprises that may show themselves in this time.

Sometimes the directee brings only confusion or a sense of emptiness. The director can be a steady witness to the availability and activity of the Spirit through all states that the directee may bring. The point of the time is not great clarity, but great willingness for God to be God, in all the unpredictable and unknowable ways that God lives in and through us. That willingness is rooted in our desire to realize the communion that is ours at every moment, whether consciously perceived or not. Often there is only a penlight's beam of insight in the darkness about that communion and our calling in it, and even that may be very hazy. Yet we can trust that we are given enough light and enough sheer trust for the steps ahead of us.

When the director sees the directee's mind struggling for what the mind always wants but very rarely receives— great clarity about God and personal calling—the director can help turn the directee toward their spiritual heart instead of remaining exclusively in their cognitive mind. In the heart we sense much but are clear about little. Even though what the heart senses doesn't have the clarity of the mind, it can have a sense of great substantiality. It can sense a moving divine force at work in our lives, however obscure this is to our minds. We are left to trust that movement and perhaps catch its tail just enough to give the mind and will something to keep them from starving, just enough to shape the next action called for. Even that much clarity may not appear in a number of sessions, in which case we can hope for a patient trust until we are given what we need to see.

The director's job is not to try and force something to come. The task is to turn to God during the session and sit in God's unknown hope for this person, wanting whatever God wants for them. Thus the director is an intercessory presence rather than an "all-knowing" presence. The direc- tor recedes into the background of God's Presence and lets whatever silence, words, or acts come from that grounded-ness. In the purest moments the director melts into God's Presence and carries the directee in selfless prayer.

Some other dimensions of what may arise in a direction session will be discussed in the next chapter on the com-munal circles of our lives.

Beginning with a New Directee •

In contemplatively oriented spiritual direction there is a desire not to reduce a directee to a series of images of them: "This is a thirty-five-year-old married Roman Catholic Irish-American urban woman with such and such personality traits and religious and social proclivities." In contemplative tradition there is a sense of the infinite mystery that we are in the image of God, along with the infinite mystery of the One whose image is in us. No set of finite images can possi-bly do justice to who we are, including our images of our-selves. The images are the tip of the great iceberg of our being, most of which is "hidden with Christ in God (Col 3:3)." We have infinite potentialities, even though only a few are called to manifest themselves extensively in this life.

The mind loves the clarity of images and concepts of identity. That is its strength. These clarities, such as are possible, show us something of our nature and direction. But the spiritual heart knows that we cannot be adequately captured in the net of these clarities. There is something precious about us that is a sacred mystery. From that deep mystery the many surprising as well as more predictable possibilities of our lives appear and show our dynamic quality, our aliveness in the living God.

Given the intrinsic inadequacies of our images and concepts, we need to hold them lightly. We can let them surround a central sense of the sacred mystery of this person who comes to us.

With this contemplatively oriented view of spiritual direction as a backdrop to meeting with a new directee, we can consider some practical aspects of beginning with someone. First of all, the rightness of even seeing a person for the first time as a possible directee needs to be brought to prayer and reflection. Do you have time to see someone at this point? Do you seem positively drawn to at least meet with this particular person for an exploratory session, or do you feel that you would be meeting only because you feel too guilty to say no?

Having decided to go forward with an exploratory session, when you come together I think that it can be valuable to begin as you would begin any future sessions: with prayer and silence, as I have already discussed. This immediately sets the tone for the meetings as times to seek the Spirit's Presence and guidance, rather than times where the director's and directee's views are exchanged apart from seeking that larger Presence throughout the session.

I think it is important to become as clear as possible about why the directee is coming to you, what they expect from the relationship, how they understand spiritual direction, and how you understand it. This shared understanding is important for both director and directee. If you do sense adequate compatibility, you are free to proceed with a common sense of purpose and process. If the directee is new to spiritual direction, they may have difficulty understanding the difference between focusing on one's relation to God and one's ego-coping concerns. In the first and future sessions, the director may need to gently bring the directee back to the former focus again and again as they unconsciously wander from it.

Sometime during the first session you may be moved to ask about the directee's sense of divine Presence in their lives and how that may seem to have changed over time. In other words, ask them something about their spiritual biography. Included here might be a question about their heart-sense of who God is for them. This may be different from their head-sense, which may be related more to what they've been conditioned by others to understand God to be but in fact do not connect with their personal experience. You might ask them to give a name or names for God that describe something of their sense of actual experience of the divine. But just as we are not fully defined by our self-images, so God is larger than any images we may have. Over time the director and directee may notice that other qualities of God's mysterious Presence show themselves in the directee's experience in ways that break open their images to larger ground.

Other potential spiritual biography questions might include: "Who have been the people in your life from whom you have picked up a living sense of God, and what is that sense?" "What has been your spiritual practice, and how has it changed over the years?" "What is happening in your life that is drawing you to spiritual direction at this time?" Other questions may well come to you during the session. Some of them can be asked, as seems appropriate, in future sessions. They don't need to be asked all at once, and I don't think it is necessary to ask them at all, except as they may illumine some current sense of the Spirit's movements.

The director might be moved to give the directee some "homework" at the end of the first session if they have not reflected on their spiritual journey before (and if you have both decided to go forward together with direction), asking them to outline the highlights of their sense of God's Spirit moving in their lives. They would not need to share this with you in the future, though, unless they felt something in it was relevant to what God seems up to at this point in their lives.

This spiritual biographical material needs to be distinguished from the directee's psychological-social biography. I don't think we need to ask them a lot about the latter. Some knowledge of it can be helpful in understanding who they are, but too much focus here tempts us to cling to the images they give as fixed labels that define the directee rather than as ones that comprise the outer surface of their being. The primary job of the director in any case is not to understand their psychic nature, as a counselor would try to do. Rather, it is to bring them to God in prayer and to join God's hope for them, beyond our understanding, as well as to protect a special time for them to listen deeply and embrace God's song in their song.

Most people probably image God very personally. Some people, though, sense the Transcendent more abstractly and impersonally—or perhaps transpersonally—in their lives. Respect for such different views of the divine is important, even as you may sense that the person needs to be open to a fuller sense of God's Presence. An impersonal sense of God may hide a fear of personal intimacy or of anthropomorphism, and a personal sense tends to hide the more awesome and uncontrollable reality of God that lies beyond secure intimate feelings. But this is speculation. The divine can be at work through every kind of image, drawing us to the living truth and way of life most needed by us. God can also be at work in our unconscious lives to this end. We do not always have to be conscious of what is happening for God to be effectively at work in us.

Sometimes in direction sessions our minds as directors might be disturbed when we feel that we have no idea what is happening with the directee or what, if anything, needs to be said. In those times we need to be given all the more to offering the person to God's light, trusting that nothing more need come from us unless it is truly given. Some of the best spiritual direction sessions, I believe, are those where the director says little or nothing, but simply prayerfully and lovingly helps secure the space for the Spirit to show itself directly to the directee or to help the directee be satisfied with the "nothing" that may be shown, trusting that the Spirit is hiddenly at work and will guide in hidden ways.

We can end the first session having been given a beginning sense of this person's life in God. You may well decide together that you need a few days to pray about whether the relationship seems called to go forward. This would be especially needed if you as director found yourself unable to be present for God, feeling very restless during the time, wanting to teach them something instead of listening, feeling great difficulty in communication. Perhaps you feel an alienness, not just a difference, in their strongly held sense of the divine, or sense other indicators of a questionable relationship.

Whether or not you decide to delay a decision to continue together, you can end the session with a brief prayer of thanksgiving and hope, led by the director, directee, or both. If we continue as director for them, a major commitment will be to offer them up in prayer again and again between sessions, wanting what God wants for them. We can sit with them in that first session and in all subsequent ones, continuing to hold up this beautiful soul in God's Light, responding in ways that we don't calculate and can't predict, the words coming from that hidden place where the director, directee, and God's Spirit overlap together.

If you do discern the rightness of entering a relationship, at the next session you might find it valuable to spell out more carefully the nature and terms of the relationship, developing a kind of *covenant* together.

This covenant can include such things as a shared sense of what the purpose of the relationship is, the role of the director, how often you will meet (normally monthly), agreeing to make a date for the next meeting before leaving a session, prayer for one another between meetings, the directee's commitment to a regular prayer practice between meetings, agreement on how long you will meet (normally for an hour), whether you will begin and end the sessions with prayer and who will lead that, the freedom to call for silence during the time, and when you will evaluate the relationship (later in this chapter I will speak about evaluation).

Confession •

In the process of a session sometimes a directee may confess one or more of their sins to you. Even though you may be in a faith tradition where only priests can formally provide absolution, if you are a layperson and are so moved, you nonetheless can quote scripture to the directee that speaks of forgiveness for repented sins. Such an act of confession in the face of God's great love reveals the freedom God has given us and embraces a sense of accountability for one's own way of life and a desire for reconciliation with God, neighbor, and self.

In a contemplative spiritual direction context, my own sense of the most fundamental sin is a willful turning away from living out of a direct connectedness with the liberating love and being of God, once we have been graced to realize that connectedness. All particular sins seem to derive from that narrowing away from the Real One toward an insulated sense of self.

The primary focus of a direction relationship, though, is on the ways in which that liberating relationship and its fruits for the world are being recognized and lived out. If a directee spends a lot of direction time focusing on a sense of guilt and unworthiness, they may not be opening to God's grace, delight, and calling for them, including the grace of forgiveness, which is meant to free us for our larger life in God. You may be called to gently draw the person's attention to this promise.

Sometimes the directee may have a sense of God that in effect is not God but rather an extension of their heavily conditioned superego. Then God primarily is seen as a judge who insists that we control our own life and get everything right. If this is the primary sense of divine reality, then the gospel of divine love and the offer of freedom and forgiveness have been missed. Such a god is out to get you at your first failing. Life is a matter of rigid conformity to the narrow path of externally defined goodness. The only reason to pay attention to such a god is because you'll die or be damned if you don't. Spiritual practices for such a person may be based primarily on fear, and may invite self-attention and judging of others by the same standards. The life-giving qualities that God's Spirit would draw out of such a person seem buried beneath this oppressive sense of God. A director needs to hold such a person in prayer and be sensitive to how the Spirit may afford opportunities to offer a more liberating view of God and self in the course of future sessions.

My guess is that most of us carry at least a streak of this sense of God as oppressive Judge in us, perhaps conditioned as children by adult authority figures who used the name of God as a means of controlling our behavior through fear. Judging indeed is one biblical dimension of God. But I take the authentic meaning of that to be a process like the one behind the modern term *tough love*. When the gentle invitations of divine love don't take hold in us, God's Spirit tries to get our attention in a firmer way. Our unloving ways are shown to have painful consequences. But this does not mean that God loves us any less. In a sense we are made of divine love; it is in the warp and woof of our being. It can be hidden from our sight, but it cannot finally disappear. Judgment in this context is a form of loving. We could say that the super-ego itself at its best carries a shadow of this love. It can be seen as a frozen memory of the kind of caring behavior that allows human beings to live together harmoniously. At its worst, though, the superego hides God's living love from us and includes views of behavior that are not made of divine love but of an overbearing human desire for control.

Evaluation •

At the beginning of the relationship the directee can be told that some time will be given for the evaluation of the relationship after a certain period of time, such as six months. When that time comes, you can save whatever amount of time seems right to you, say twenty minutes, at the end of a session to reflect together on such things as:

a. how grace seems to have shown itself in the relation-ship;

b. what it is about the way the director questions, speaks, prays, and is silent that seems to assist or hinder the directee's presence for God;

c. whether it truly feels right to continue.

Both people need to be just as honest about these questions as possible. This reflection might best emerge out of several minutes of silence so that what is said comes as much as possible out of a sense of the Spirit.

There need be no sense of failure or guilt if the situation does not feel right, either on the part of the director or the directee. There is a particular mysterious chemistry and timing in direction relationships that prove to be either right or wrong at a given time in a person's life. The "best" spiritual director for someone may be the "worst" spiritual director for another person. This doesn't mean that we always need to feel comfortable with each other. There may be a challenge in a relationship that's called for. But if the relationship has a way of regularly leaving either person unfree to be present for God when necessary, then it needs to end. If that happens and the directee wants to continue in spiritual direction and doesn't know of other directors, the director may be able to supply some names of people or centers that could serve as resources in finding an appropriate person.

If it does seem right to continue, you can review the terms of your covenant together and agree to have an evaluation again at the request of either person, probably at least once a year.

The Question of Payment •

Many directors and directees are uncertain about how to approach the sometimes delicate issue of contribution to the director. Given the personal and spiritual issues potentially involved and the little writing that has been done about it to my knowledge, I am going to go into this area in some detail.

There is a long history of some kind of material "thank you" for spiritual guidance in all or most of the world's major religious traditions. In Christian tradition this practice has taken the form of contributions to a charity of the director's, to the religious community of the director, or sometimes to the director her-/himself. Normally this has involved a "free-will" offering, often some material gift other than money, such as a book or food. The staffs of churches are already supported by free-will offerings of members for the overall work of the church, normally including any spiritual guidance that might be given.

Today the situation is affected by two relatively new elements:

1. The growth of psychological counseling, which usually involves a fee-for-service basis. Some counselors now are also providing spiritual direction. The wide availability of such counseling has conditioned people in general to a fee-for-service model.
2. The rise of laypersons as spiritual directors, who have no salaried base in a religious organization and sometimes nowhere else as well.

Individual directors demonstrate a legitimate range of opinion about this issue. I will simply lay them out along a continuum. Many of the comments are a compendium of views stated by others. I will leave it to you to discern where you stand in terms of your values and situation.

1. *No Contributions.* Spiritual direction models free grace. It should not be the means of one's support. If there is a payment, the director may be tempted to be "helpful," to make something happen that in his or her eyes merits payment, rather than leaning back into God and listening with the directee for *God's* help. From the directee's side, payment of the director may engender a subtle, unreasonable expectation regarding the director.

2. *Limited Contribution.* Frequently an individual will want to make a contribution out of such motivations as accountability, obligation, and gratitude. The director and directee should be free to discern together what is best. Such a payment could be either to a religious organization to which the director belongs or to some charity or other religious community probably designated by the director. The only payment appropriate for the director would be an occasional spontaneous thank-you gift, normally a small nonmonetary offering of some kind.

3. *Fee for Service.* If a director takes time from paid work, or takes a lower-paid or no outside job in order to do direction, he or she may need a contribution for their own and their family's basic support. In a culture that is so conditioned to value what is paid for, the relationship might be taken more seriously by some people if there is a fee involved. Ask for a free-will offering or for a reasonable suggested amount, perhaps on a sliding scale, and be sure not to exclude anyone who cannot pay nor to treat in a better way those who do pay.

Boundaries in the Relationship[1] •

The basic question concerning boundaries in a spiritual direction relationship I believe is this: What boundaries will support our mutual freedom for God in the direction session? Our answers will likely be a bit different with each directee. We especially need to respect the boundaries that each directee sets in the relationship. We may see these changing somewhat over time, as trust between you and the directee grows.

As an example, let me talk about the boundary of sexual activity. The spiritual direction relationship often involves a special quality of intimacy and vulnerability. On one level, since the focus is on God rather than on the other person, there is less likelihood of psychological transference and other emotional enmeshment with the other person than would be true in a counseling relationship. On another level, though, the intimate spiritual affections exposed in the relationship can affect our sense of the other person. You may come to feel the beauty of the directee's soul, and/or the directee may connect you with their affection for God. Accompanying such an awareness may be a new sense of the physical beauty of the other person. He or she may become magnetized, erotically attractive to you.

Frequently, we see only two choices: either to suppress such feelings quickly (perhaps scolding ourselves as we do) or to act on them. Let me suggest a third option in this delicate, powerful arena of attraction—that is, simple *appreciation* of the feeling without judging it, identifying with it, or acting on it. Then, the feeling is free to waft through us just as it is. We are more able to experience it as a natural reverberation of this person's soul-beauty; we can let it be what it is with greater simplicity. I realize this is not easy, partly because this way of being has not normally been an option in our cultural conditioning. But I think it is a valuable alternative for us rather than either deadening our feelings or being driven to act on them.

If we try to deaden our feelings—whatever their content—I wonder if this response doesn't also deaden our real openness, our immediate givenness to God in the moment. Allowing *appreciation* rather than deadening can enable us to be more appreciative of God's vibrant, alluring quality alive in the moment. If, however, we find ourselves significantly and often distracted by a magnetized, erotic feeling toward the directee, and/or the directee has such a feeling toward us, I believe that the freedom for God that is needed in authentic spiritual direction has been lost, and the relationship needs to be ended. In any case, it's important to realize that directors are often in a position of subtle power with directees, who have given the directors their trust and vulnerable presence before God. That position must never be exploited by the director, sexually or otherwise.

Physical touch that is not bound up with erotic attraction, I think, can have an authentic place in a spiritual direction session. It can provide a kind of embodiment of invisible divine caring presence. This might include a handshake at the beginning and/or end of a session, holding the directee's hands in prayer together, or a light hand on their back or a hug as they are leaving. But discretion is important here. Some people have great difficulty with physical touch and their desire for physical distance needs to be respected. Sometimes this even means we need to sit a little farther away from a particular directee than we might with someone whose freedom for God in the session is not impeded by close physical proximity. We need to have a sense of their explicit or implicit permission for any kind of physical intimacy. With some people the relationship may rightly never include any kind of physical touch.

Some people have a need for unusually tight boundaries stemming from experiences of abuse and exploitation earlier in their lives. We need to be sensitive to such people's fears and needs for boundaries in direction relationships. To the extent that people experience difficulty in setting their own boundaries, they are frequently tempted to test a director's boundaries (by asking him/her to dinner, to lengthen the session, to meet more frequently, etc.). The director then needs to be the initiator in setting boundaries. Anything that diverts attention from God to the director can interfere with mutual freedom for God in the relationship.

No one wants to live with *unnecessary* boundaries. Everyone yearns somewhere deep down for a quality of fulfilling intimacy, of spontaneous interrelatedness. When we are most graced to be in the fullness of our souls, such spontaneous interrelatedness is more free from fear-induced boundaries. In such graced times we reflect a little more of the dance of the Holy Trinity, in whose image Christian tradition says we are made and wherein each member flows into the other without loss of itself, a true unity in diversity. I think we all know what it is like to have tasted such a heavenly relationship, however brief it may have been. But we usually spend much more time in either mildly disconnected or possessive and grasping modes of relating.

Because of this, we need both the "law" and the "gospel" of spiritual direction.

The "law" of spiritual direction is concerned with any violation of the dignity and/or freedom of the directee. This includes avoidance of such things as sexual suggestiveness or activity, unwanted probing into sensitive parts of directees' lives, violation of confidence, ignoring time commitments for meeting, and shifting the ultimate locus of discernment of what's happening and how to respond away from the directee to the director (at least in the nonguru model of direction advocated in this book and in most spiritual direction programs with which I am familiar today). This last "law," I believe, is particularly important in relation to whatever may come through you as spiritual director in a session. No matter how much you may believe that what you say or do comes from God, the *ultimate* discerner of that, I think, must be the directee, not the director.

When God's Spirit is moving in the same way in both people, in effect there will be a *shared* discernment, a shared sense of what is happening and what is called for, a mutual confirmation. When such sharing is not present, the director can question the directee and give her/his view of things, but not cross the line into demanding that the directee see things in the same way. We're dealing with the great mystery of God in a person's life, and we need to respect God's often mysterious ways. Attempts at overclarity or overguidance in a session can reflect the director's anxiety over bearing the mystery of this person's soul and allowing it to evolve step by mysterious step, beyond our control and clarity.

As valuable as the "law" of spiritual direction is, it needs to be seen in the light of the "gospel." The gospel of spiritual direction is our trust in the Holy Spirit's liberating, uniting presence and our empowered willingness for whatever the Spirit spontaneously gives in the sessions for the sake of the directee's fullness of soul. The law is ultimately to support this gospel.

A direction relationship needs to have a sense of safety on the human level—a sense that the director will not violate the directee's integrity. Such a sense of human safety, however, is a platform for a sense of *daring,* not timidity, with *God* in the direction session—a sense of room where our desire and God's desire for an expansiveness of soul can live, even at the price of discomfort and disorientation on the ego level. I might add that expansiveness of soul here doesn't refer only to affective experience. It also includes unfelt and empty experience, where one trusts the expanse of emptiness as part of an expansive soul. Emptiness in this sense is not the absence of God; it is simply experiencing God in a way with which we are not so familiar, experiencing God emptied of our normal ways of understanding spiritual experience.

Different Means of Presence for Spiritual Direction •

We can be present for people's spiritual life in ways other than in-person one-on-one or group spiritual direction. There is a centuries-old tradition of spiritual direction by correspondence. This means provides an opportunity for carefully considered reflection, but it has the disadvantages of not allowing dialogue together. The same could be said for a relationship through audiotape. In addition to tapes, modern technology has opened up other avenues. Some people "meet" on the telephone. This offsets the disadvantages of correspondence but loses the fullness of presence that in-person contact offers. Many individuals, however, may feel just the opposite: they may find physical presence distracting and are more able to be present for God and for other people by telephone.

The same could be said for those who meet through e-mail. The potential knowledge and stimulus to prayer that can come from a person's way of speaking and being present are lost. If this online time is not done at an agreed-upon hour of the day when there is an immediate back-and-forth communication, there is the advantage of both persons communicating at a time when they feel particularly ready, since an e-mail from a directee could be received and not responded to until one felt in the best prayerful readiness to respond. If the time gap is too long, however, like spiritual direction by correspondence, your response may no longer be relevant to the directee's evolving life in the Spirit.

We could tag certain books, articles, tapes, talks, and sermons about the spiritual life as indirect means of spiritual companionship for many people. These are more like general monologues that don't arise from a specific relationship with the person seeking spiritual companionship, and of course there normally is no dialogue. Nonetheless, the Spirit sometimes uses these "voices" to carry a word to us that seems to just fit our situation at the moment. They can lead us to a sense of the Spirit at work in, through, and around us.

Where Is It All Leading? •

Over time the director will likely sense the spiraling spiritual journey of the directee in all its shadings. In that spiral we are attending what Gregory of Nyssa in the early church called the twofold nature of our vocation. My own words for this calling are: (1) to realize our end-in-itself loving union with God, and (2) to let God's Spirit flow through our unique gifts and situations in the world in ways that serve God's kindom of shalom.

This calling is lifelong and full of twists and turns in the way it evolves. Someone may seem to return to where they had been, but in fact they may be retouching an old place with new eyes and freedom. However helpful historical or modern attempts to describe stages of the spiritual life can be to give us a broad sense of what can happen over a lifetime, no such scheme can ever be adequate, because we are dealing with the surprising and unique ways of grace in each human life.[2] Because of this dynamic quality of the spiritual life, there is no necessary end to the need for a spiritual companion. As I have alluded to earlier, we are never "finished" images of God in this life. We are always on the frontier of the living Spirit in each new moment. The moments are bound together by the desire God places in us to realize the fullness of God in life, however disguised this desire may be in more finite desires at a given time.

After many years of an intentional spiritual journey we may come to a point where we seem to have internalized so much sensitivity to the ways of the Spirit in us that we feel less need to talk about them with someone else. My own sense, though, is that at least occasional opportunities with a mature spiritual friend to test our senses of what is happening spiritually is important in helping to guard us from illusion while giving someone else a chance to encourage our life in God and pray for us.

Support for the Spiritual Director's Presence to God for Directees: The Value of Director Peer Groups

If we're offering ongoing spiritual companionship for others, it is vital to be willing to meet with some group of other directors with whom we can reflect on the way we are being present to God for our directees. Such a meeting gives us opportunity to share both our difficulties and our appreciation for what is happening in the relationships.

Over the years of developing such groups at the Shalem Institute we have come to see the great value of providing a prayerful atmosphere for mutual listening to the Spirit in these meetings, as opposed to a more objective, analytical atmosphere. In other words, we encourage the meeting itself to model the atmosphere of a spiritual direction session, where head and spiritual heart are together.

Such a group ideally will have four to six members from different faith traditions. All of them will be actively engaged in offering spiritual direction, and each will have a spiritual director for themselves. The group can meet monthly, with two people prepared to present themselves in relation to a directee each time. The convener/process facilitator for the meetings can be rotated among members.

The presenters at a given meeting present themselves in relation to a directee (whose identity is kept confidential), saying just enough about the directee to provide a context for looking at the presenter's questions about themselves. The task of the group then is not to give them advice for their directees, whom the group members do not know, but rather to let emerge from their prayerful listening to the presenters whatever shows itself in the way of questions or wonderings concerning the presenter's faith, prayer, struggles, fears, and hopes in the relationship. Put another way, the members are wanting to listen for what the Spirit sees as important for the person to hear, for their own sake and for their directees' sake.

In the process of a peer-group meeting, anyone in the group can call for silence at any time, whenever someone feels that the group has become too grasping or speedy, eclipsing a listening-to-God presence. These silences give everyone an opportunity to lean back into the Spirit's presence and let whatever may show itself from that deeper, freer, prayerful place. The spiritual vulnerability found in such a peer-group atmosphere reinforces this way of being present when we are with directees. Every member of such a group usually benefits from such meetings, whether they are presenters or not. The Spirit has a way of circulating its gifts among the members of the group, just as it does between director and directee.

An outline for looking at the intent and process for a two-hour meeting of such a group, based on the peer-group process used at the Shalem Institute, is included in appendix B.

On occasion a director may need a confidential *consultation* with a trusted resource person about a particular direction situation. For example, you may note that a heavy psychological issue continues to be raised, and you want to consult with a therapist as to whether or not you should suggest that the directee receive some counseling. Or your directee continues to speak of feeling oppressed by a demonic force, and you want to consult with someone who has more background in the area of the demonic. If this consultation would involve divulging anything that could possibly reveal who the directee is, it is important that the director receive permission from the directee before proceeding. In a spiritual direction peer group the director normally gives only a few bare facts about the directee as a background. The anonymity of the directee must be preserved at all costs, even if this requires changing the gender or other particulars of the person in the description.

CHAPTER 7

HOW DO WE ATTEND THE COMMUNAL CIRCLES OF OUR LIVES?

Social Contexts for Spiritual Direction •

We are always living in community, with God and with God's creatures. Even when we are alone in the woods or the desert, we are surrounded by living creatures, and our minds are often full of people who are not present. This chapter will examine a range of the communities in which we live as they are relevant to spiritual direction, looking especially for the ways they can mediate and blind us to divine presence, the ways they can be icons or idols for us.

Gender

Male and female God made them...in God's image. (Gen 1:27)

One comes to the spiritual direction relationship, among other identities, as a woman or as a man. We feel the life we have been given through a male or female body, a gendered body that has its own distinctive biological, psychological, and cultural conditioning. Just what intrinsic differences there may be, beyond the obvious biological ones, are issues of great controversy and uncertainty. I have been leery of making generalizations about these differences, because I find many exceptions to those that have been posited by others. In the spiritual life, at least, I believe that the differences between us are much more quantitative than qualitative. St. Paul speaks of being "in Christ" as a quality that is neither male nor female (Gal 3:28). Nonetheless, there are some valuable questions to which we can be sensitive concerning individual gender experience, questions that we may find helpful to ask ourselves, and to be aware of in listening to others.

1. *What distinctive experience as a woman or man (physically, psychologically, and/or culturally) do you bring to God in prayer?*

We might find that this gender-influenced experience affects the way we understand and relate to God. We also can find that we don't have to be locked into that way if it inadequately reflects our calling. For example, a man once told me that when he went on retreat, he always felt that he had to bring God some product, assuming that God expected a performance from him as everyone else did in his life, an expectation that he felt related to his personal conditioning as a man. Finally, after some years of spiritual deepening, he found himself able to just be with God on retreat, realizing that God didn't expect anything more of him than an end-in-itself friendship during that time. His sense of spiritual manhood had expanded now to include not only a sense of doing for God, but a capacity for simply being with God.

We could conjecture here (supported by at least one research study) that most males as children learn to relate to one another primarily through *doing* something together, whereas most females as children learn to relate to one another primarily through *sharing secrets.* As this performance versus relational intimacy difference is reinforced over the years in various arenas of life, it might help to explain why the majority of people who come for spiritual direction—and for any other activity that focuses on our direct, intimate relationship with God—seem to be women. For many men, being God's strong "lieutenant" in some church, charitable, sport, or community-building project might feel like a more comfortable extension of their normal way of positively relating than in being God's lover. But this doesn't mean that they are incapable of being such a lover, as the lyrical writings of many male mystics throughout history have demonstrated. The context for such loving for many men, though, may be more often in solitude (e.g., while fishing or walking in the woods), where the spiritual awareness that appears is not often shared with other people.

While holding up the potential of such a personal relationship with male directees, the director also needs to affirm the equal value of their potential "lieutenant" activities. If more men are to be brought into appreciation of God's active, guiding Presence, there needs to be more appreciation of that Presence in the masculine qualities they have been given by God, rather than assuming that these are inferior to "feminine" traits.[1]

2. *When you reflect on your sense of God over the years at the heart level of your experience (i.e., before you begin cognitively interpreting it),* do you sense God as more masculine, *feminine, inclusively personal, transpersonal, or impersonal? Has this been consistent or different at different times?*

It is important here to realize the difference between spontaneously given images or senses of God, those that more truly reflect our experience, and conceptually conveyed images that have been conditioned in us through others, as I mentioned earlier. For example, we may be used to naming the divine as "Father" or "Christ," and these may indeed reflect our actual experience, but they may not. Our immediate experience may be of a radiant lightness, or perhaps a nurturing or even erotic woman. In spiritual direction we want to stay as close to people's actual experience as possible. This means that we can be affirming of original names for God spoken by the directee, if these best describe a person's actual experience of the divine presence—or no names if their experience is formless. Sometimes we may be moved to note a connection between the name given by a directee and a similar or same name given in scripture or by a great saint, of which the individual is unaware. This can leave the person sensing some confirmation of their experience in spiritual tradition.

I think that the foundational scriptural revelation of God's nature is one of loving, guiding light. However, scriptural and later church tradition concerning God's nature and our relationship to God can also reflect cultural patterns that contribute to our uncertainty and confusion—rather than our enlightenment—about God's nature. In scripture, for example, God can be portrayed as a tribal, male, warlike deity ruthlessly slaying the enemies of Israel, and yet also as a shepherd tenderly caring for the sheep, along with many other images connected with the culture of Israel.

An example of a culturally related postbiblical tradition (partly inspired by biblical precedent) of imaging the divine-human relationship would be classical bridal mysticism reflected in many medieval writers. This imagery usually depicts the human soul as the bride of Christ, and God as Father of the bride. For all its intimacy and beauty, such imagery can have a downside for women and men. For women, the imagery may reflect some of their direct experience of the holy, but insofar as it implies the subordination of the feminine to the masculine, as was normal in medieval culture, it also may contradict women's sense of call from God to a life of equality and initiative along with men. It is also unsupportive of women's experience of the divine in feminine form.

Contemporary literature has dealt extensively with these dimensions of women's images of God.[2] I would like to speculate a little here about a dimension of the relation of the masculine to the feminine that I have not found receiving adequate attention in spiritual literature: the masculine attraction to the feminine. For some men, at least, I think that the imagery of their own souls as feminine and God as masculine, as portrayed in traditional bridal mysticism, ignores or denies their powerful experience of the mysterious, alluring otherness in life found in the adult, erotic woman. Indeed, I know of no positive, sacred image of such a woman in Christian tradition (as opposed to a nonerotic image of the Blessed Virgin Mary and of many female saints).

I have known men who have had surprising and powerful interior encounters with the divine in the form of an alluring feminine presence (just as I know women whose encounter has been in the form of an alluring masculine presence). These men had no place in Christian spiritual tradition, so far as I am aware, where they could positively connect such an experience of divine presence. The scriptural texts that use an intimate male/female metaphor for the divine/human relationship, such as Hosea and the Song of Songs, focus on the divine as masculine and the human as feminine, or the divine as maternally feminine, as when Jesus laments over Jerusalem (Matt 23:37).

On a more everyday level, when heterosexual men see a beautiful woman, they find little or nothing positive in the tradition with which to connect it. On the contrary, they find much about the allures of women that will distract them from God. With such a "blackout" of their positive erotic feelings toward women in Christian tradition, at least outside of marriage, men are easily left with a sense that this powerful feeling in them felt toward many women has nothing to do with God, thus depriving them of one way God may be appearing to them in the moment. The eros of the feminine is historically left outside the realm of holy encounter, except guardedly within the confines of marriage. The experience is often "secularized" as lust and loses its potentially reverential dimension. It then becomes simply a physical attraction to suppress or indulge.

In the last chapter I alluded to a third possibility between either suppressing or indulging our erotic attraction to another person. This entails letting that erotic energy be transformed into an appreciation of God's beauty and presence in the other person, drawing us toward God rather than toward sexual possession of that person. This option, to my knowledge, is rarely if ever encouraged in the tradition. One result is that the erotic dimension of men's feelings for women is degraded as a potential avenue of the Spirit, and the erotic woman in general is degraded as a spiritual being (we could say the same thing about women's attraction to men). I am aware that erotic feelings can be very powerful, and I think there has been a basically right instinct in human society that these must be carefully controlled for the sake of social order and familial stability. However, if this sense of a third, spiritually grounded option to suppression or acted-out sexual expression is carefully offered, there might be room for more appreciation of the Spirit's involvement in our feelings, even as we maintain a clear sense of boundaries in terms of acting on those feelings.

Some form of *bridegroom* mysticism perhaps is needed as an option for many men, wherein they can legitimately affirm an experience of a masculine soul being lured to deeper love of God by a feminine sense of God's presence, both in their interior experience of the divine and in their experience of women. Such an option may have a surprising, positive effect on men's deeper opening to the spiritual life and recognition of the ways God can appear to them.[3]

GENDER RELATIONSHIP IN DIRECTION

Besides being sensitive to the potential masculine and feminine influence on a person's relationship with God, the director needs to be aware of the impact of the directee's gender on the direction relationship itself. If, for example, there is a strong, steady erotic attraction, fear, or anger clicked off in either director or directee in such a way that one or the other or both lose their freedom for spacious listening presence to God in each other's presence, then it is likely that termination is called for.

On the other hand, the very otherness of a person of opposite gender can provide a positive stimulus and spaciousness for relating to the mysterious Otherness of God. Carl Jung made much of the ways we find a missing dimension of our own being through the otherness of the opposite gender. We could say that a dimension of God's Spirit is potentially revealed to us through a differently gendered person, a dimension that we yearn to include in our own sense of full identity. When we read in Genesis 1:27 that God created us in the divine image, male and female, we could imply that the divine image is revealed *between* men and women in a distinctive way. Many great spiritual friendships in Christian history have been between women and men.

However, this does not often appear to be true of marital relationships in spiritual literature; these relationships are loaded with many expectations and emotional dynamics that can make it as difficult for spouses to be spiritual directors (as opposed to informal spiritual friends) as to be therapists for one another. I will return to these relationships in the section on household spirituality.

For persons who are well down the road toward spiritual maturity, in the sense of being graced with a liberated primary identity in God (or at least the desire for it) in the presence of the ego self, other people, things, and nature, it probably makes little difference whether the spiritual friend is male or female. For such people these dimensions of self and God have become so integrated, or at least transcended, that almost anyone can serve as a transparency for the Holy One. The relative unimportance of the friend's gender is underlined when we remember that the primary relationship in spiritual direction is between God and the spiritual friend, not between the friends themselves. However, individuals with deeply conditioned psychological barriers with men or women, even if they are relatively mature spiritually, may find themselves gravitating toward someone of the gender that allows them to be most free for God during the meeting time.

DIRECTION ISSUES RELATED TO SEXUAL IDENTITY

Homosexually (both men and women) and bisexually oriented directees usually share a sense of marginalization in society and the church, and have often experienced much suffering because of their orientation, even as we live in a time of greater acceptance by a growing percentage of the heterosexual majority. As is so often true with marginalized people of any kind, these individuals often have been pressed deeper in their consideration of the meaning of life and the ways of God with them. They need to have their orientation folded into their sense of God's love for them and to sense the director's acceptance, especially if the director is not similarly oriented. The erotic dimensions of sexuality need to be seen in the light of God's view of creation declared in Genesis to be "good." Otherwise they can remain hidden and feared in a direction relationship, even though the Spirit may be moving in this dimension of the directee's life and the directee feels the need to reflect on what that movement is showing.[4]

In relation to sexuality, as with any other area of life, the direction relationship may or may not be a called-for arena for reflection. The director does not have to be privy to every area of a directee's life as a matter of course. There would never be time for that in one hour a month in any case. What is important, though, is that the director be available to listen and talk openly about any area of life raised by the directee where there is a desire to sense the Spirit's movement in it at this point in his or her life. As the area of homosexuality or bisexuality is raised by a directee, I think the director's fundamental open-to-God stance and likely basic questions would be largely the same as with a heterosexual directee, though with a special sensitivity to the cultural marginalization and pain felt by so many non-heterosexual people.

Here are some examples of questions that might sensitize the director to specifically spiritual dimensions of sexuality (both heterosexual and homosexual), as opposed to more ego-coping counseling dimensions. I am not advocating that these questions be asked by the director, but they may form a helpful backdrop for your prayerful presence to this arena as it is raised. The form of any questions that you do ask hopefully will come out of your leaning openly into God in the moment, rather than from any predetermined list of questions.

① How do your sexual feelings and behaviors affect your relationship to God at a given time? For example, can you let God in on your feelings, action choices, and desire for acceptance, or is your attention captured, diverted from open availability to God?

2. Does another loved person become a displacement for God, someone you look to in order to ultimately secure yourself, thus becoming in effect an idol, or is the other person more of an icon for you, someone you see as a particular shaping and gift of a larger divine Love that is not confined to this person or any other?

3. Are you able to open your behavior with another person to God in such a way that you are willing to be guided by what you are shown is most lovingly called for in the whole context of the situation? For example, if you are shown that your behavior knowingly interferes with others' relation to God or otherwise harms or exploits other people, are you willing for repentance and forgiveness, or if it is harmful compulsive behavior, for therapy or group help of some kind?

4. Are you more identified with your ego-self, including, for example, an image of "homosexual" or "straight," than you are identified with your deeper, larger identity in God?

5. Can you give priority to the compassionate energy of God in you? This energy, I believe, is intrinsically an open quality of loving energy that in erotic turning to a particular person becomes magnetized, yet can still retain an open compassionate quality. This quality can be an icon for God's loving presence with another person.

Homosexual and bisexual people can stir up a lot of confused, difficult feelings in heterosexual people, just as heterosexuals can in homosexuals and bisexuals. Sometimes this tension is full of grace in the way it leads us to face and accept the larger mystery of erotic feelings that are bestowed on ourselves and others. It is helpful to remember that human beings are born with a capacity for erotic feelings with either sex. We later find ourselves at varying places on a continuum in terms of our erotic responses to people of the same and opposite sex related to a scientifically unclear combination of genetic and conditioned factors beyond our control. Thus it is not a simple matter of being either homosexual, bisexual, or heterosexual. We are first of all human beings made in the image of God, who happen to have a range of different proclivities in our erotic attractions as in other areas of our lives, just as we happen to be made male or female.

We might agree to disagree with a directee about what we may believe God has given as normative erotic behavior as opposed to simply culturally standard behavior. Scripture, tradition, and the churches have different theologically and culturally influenced views about the delicate area of nonheterosexual relationships. Jesus says nothing directly about it. We are finally left to prayerfully discern which of these views seem most compatible with the gospel of divine love.

As directors I think our key task is to be available to God for the directee in the area of their sexuality as this may be raised, wanting *them* to be available for God, too, as together you listen for the guidance of the Spirit. The director can stay as director for a person as long as they are able to remain open to God with that person and not be so fascinated or disturbed by the directee's sexual orientation and activity that they cannot be an open channel for God's guiding presence.

Let me end this section by saying that I think we need to hold up the giftedness of our differences. As women and men (whether heterosexual, homosexual, or bisexual) we are created in a complementary relationship to one another, a partnership. We reflect the diversity in unity of the Holy Trinity itself, wherein we see a mutual emptying into one another, an indwelling of one another, without loss of personal identity. We are meant to realize the new

community in Christ, an inclusive community of recipro-
cal love and complementary service. Such a community is
good news for men and women of every sexual orientation.

Household Spirituality

Most people spend a great deal of their lives with parents,
siblings, spouses, lifetime partners, and/or children. A few
people also spend much time within a residential religious
community. These long-term covenanted relationships at
their best are windows through which God's love and calling
come to us, and through us. Their longevity and covenanted
quality encourage our sense of steady connectedness and care
for life beyond our own. This long-term quality can also turn
relationships into an ascetical arena where our hard and
delusory edges are exposed and worn down as we are
stretched by the sheer otherness of those with whom we live.

Such households at their best can be intentional households of faith, little domestic churches where the spiritual
dimension of daily experience and activity is consciously
recognized and embraced in an atmosphere of respect for
the different ways individuals may approach and be touched
by the divine. Often, though, directees will come with a
sense of spiritual frustration about their households. Others
in the household may have no conscious sense of God's reality in their lives, or if they do, it is a very different sense than
that of the directee. The very center of the directees' lives,
their way of relating to God, is not appreciated or shared
by others. Directees are tempted to go beyond sadness to a
subtle contempt for the spouse or other household members,
believing themselves to be spiritually superior.

The director can help the directee consider that God is
involved with every person's life in God's own way. Even if
we assume that the other person is not living a consciously
spiritual life, we can trust that God is still lovingly at work

with them. Maybe other members of the household are being moved by God in ways different from those of the directee. They, like us, may or may not be very aware of or responsive to the subtle leadings of the Spirit, yet we can trust that those leadings are there. The very differences between the directee and other household members may have a way of spiritually stretching the directee to a larger sense of God's reality. This awareness does not completely relieve the pain of such situations, since we all yearn to have others near us with whom we can share what is deepest in our lives. But it at least can provide some value and hope in painful circumstances.

The household can become a substitute for God by becoming the place of our central identity, purpose, and security. Such a focus can be dangerous. One of the major battles in the world today is the one between a sense of being owned by a genetic family, larger clan, or ethnic group versus having an identity that transcends these ties. Such ownership is enshrined in many national legal systems and ethnic customs in a variety of ways. This sense of being possessed by a group can have the positive effects engendering an ordered and caring way of life together with a sense of mutual responsibility. Such an orientation also challenges the kind of narcissistic individualism that can result when there is neither a sense of family attachment nor any other form of transcendent identity.

On the negative side, however, such a sense of possession can be constrictive of a person's calling to a larger identity and life in God, and to the larger human family. Historically we read of many family battles ensuing from a family member's claim to a spiritual identity and vocation that transcends and perhaps challenges family and ethnic priorities.

Jesus was ensconced in a culture with a powerful sense of family and ethnic identity. He was shockingly revolutionary when he called us to transcend family identity and see our foundational parenting in God and foundational community with those who yearn for God (Matt 12:49). Jesus affirmed the societally sanctioned family in his hallowing of marriage, but this affirmation is kept relative to the larger calling to and identity with God's universal community of shalom that is breaking in among us through the power of the Holy Spirit. The household can be a respected, graced expression of God's life for us, but it is not an end in itself. It is an incubator for life in a larger human and divine community. Part of the asceticism of family life is the willingness to eventually give up children to this larger community rather than trying to keep their primary identity and mission within the family.

Spiritual direction tries to give space for a person to be attuned to God's Spirit very directly, and it assumes that nothing is sacred but that which is truly of God. In spiritual direction the value of any social structure in which the directee may be involved is related to its capacity to reflect the loving, just nature of God. Where this is not happening, where it is grossly violated, spiritual direction can have a prophetic quality. It can be an arena where a person recognizes the call to ask God to help change a relationship to reflect the nature of love, and where this does not prove possible, to be free to leave it. Thus spiritual direction is not meant to be a way of propping up uncalled for, unloving, unjust, oppressively restrictive social structures; rather, it can provide an opportunity to test the structures in which we are involved for their reflection of God's way for us.

In this sense authentic spiritual direction inevitably is on the fringe of religious, household, or any other social structure. It shows us that we finally are not subject to any power but the power of God's Spirit at work in us, understood in the light of mature spiritual tradition. At the same time spiritual direction is attending the very heart of all social structures in a very caring way. It is attending that which is Spirit-given about them and what that divine Spirit is calling for through us to help those structures to reverberate God's vision for us.

When we are working with a married directee, the direction relationship may be felt as a blessing for the marriage as it enhances a person's confidence in God's loving involvement in all dimensions of living and relationship. On the other hand, the direction relationship may be felt as a potential threat to the spouse. Spiritual direction can be a very intimate experience, and a spouse might feel some competition, especially if he or she feels insecure in the marriage or somehow unable to be a cotraveler on an intentional and shared spiritual journey with their partner.

Sometimes both spouses will ask to be in direction with the same director (at different meeting times). This may work out, but it can have special problems. For example, one spouse may say things about the other spouse, leaving the director with knowledge that cannot be shared with the other spouse yet affects the director's way of seeing that person. Also, one spouse may feel subtly competitive in terms of their own spiritual experience compared to their spouse's.

Following are a few questions to which directors might be sensitive as the directee's household context may be brought up in a direction relationship. As with the questions at the end of the last section, I am not listing these as ones to ask directees, but just as examples of spiritual concerns in the household.

1. How is the directee's relationship with God reflected in their relationships with family, spouse, and/or significant others? Is their relationship with these people ever addressed in their prayer?

2. To what does the directee feel the Spirit is calling them in household relationships at this point in their lives? Does this feel like a different kind of calling than that shown in relation-ships with spiritual companions outside the household?

3. How does the directee's commitment to spiritual direc-tion seem to affect their relationship with household mem-bers? If this is an area of concern, what has shown itself to you about it when you bring it to prayer?

Workplace Spirituality

Work gives us a special sense of purpose and structure in our lives. It can take many forms, such as work for pay, vol-unteer work, and homemaking. All forms of work offer a spiritual paradox. On the one hand, work can be seen as a particular arena of divine vocation and presence. Even if the work is being done out of economic necessity and doesn't feel like it's what we are most gifted and called to be doing, it can be seen as an arena of service that can be done to the glory of God. God's Spirit can be seen to be present in any work, energizing whatever is worthwhile in it.

On the other hand, even if we follow scripture and say that work is God-given, something in us and certainly in our cul-ture lends testimony to the fact that work is done on our own. We may do it for God, but *we* are the ones doing it. What we do is seen as a separate act. God is not immediately involved. We are on our own. God is a remote background, but not an imminent Presence. A contemplative perspective would challenge this view. It would say that work does not create some screen that separates us from God. Rather, God is just as much present in the workplace as anywhere else in life. God is the immediate ground of all possibilities and hopeful-ness in our work. We can turn to that ground and let it give immediate perspective, freedom, and compassion to the work at hand. It can be a divine/human cocreation.

Directees may raise many issues about God in the work-place. These may involve such things as personal vocation,

justice, relationships, organizational values, decision making, and personal spiritual practice on the job. Some
directees may talk almost exclusively about their work;
others may never mention it, and the director may feel
called to question how it relates to their spiritual journey.
As with anything else raised by the directee, the director's
first call is to let God in on the "work" of the spiritual
direction session by immediately leaving space for God to
enter: opening oneself to what one does not know; inviting
God to fill that unknowing as God will, even if it is filled
with nothing. If nothing is given, then perhaps that is a
sign that whatever needs to come will be directly through
the directee or that it is not yet time for anything to be
given at all, and the situation needs to steep in patient trust
for a while.

With this fundamental orientation of the director as
steady grounding, there are some particular areas of sensitivity concerning the workplace that the director can
keep in mind. The most important, I believe, concerns the
paradox mentioned above: directees can see work as God-
given and yet not have a sense of God's direct involvement. As it seems right, directors might encourage
directees to turn to the divine ground of work in the
moments of the workday. Directees can be asked if there
are ways that this happens most naturally for them. The
following examples may help give the director a sense of a
certain range of possibilities:

1. *Looking periodically at a particular object in your place
of work that has a way of reminding you of the larger Presence.*
This might be an object with specific faith meaning that is
set up, such as an icon, cross, or candle, or it might be a
special object from nature, such as a stone or picture of a
sunset or ocean. It also might involve looking directly at

mindfulness

something in nature (if you work outside or have a window) such as the sky or a tree.

2. *From time to time throughout the day, touching some object you have on your person.* This might be something like a cross or bracelet that you wear, or a special object in your pocket, or placing your hand on your heart.

3. *Letting rise a particular word of scripture or a mantralike repeated phrase such as the Jesus Prayer, or some particular interior image.*

4. *Reading briefly from scripture or other spiritual writings at certain times.* A similarly effective practice is taking time for a brief prayer (whether it be read, recited from memory, or spontaneously formed on the spot). Such a prayer should express your openness for God's direct guidance in the work of the day. A tape could be used instead of reading. It might include some special music that draws you to the Presence.

5. *Intercession for particular people and situations in the workplace.* This might include a dedication of one's work to God on a given day for the sake of some particular people or situation.

6. *Without the necessity of adding anything, simply, immediately appreciating the spacious, available, divine Love that flows in this work moment just as it is, no matter what is happening.* This is an inner orientation in the process of working rather than a separate act of any kind. It is an orientation that is open and yielding to the flow of grace in the moment, an intimate "practicing of the Presence."

Sometimes directees may feel called to take some particular action related to a situation of injustice, harmful relationships, frustrating organizational policies, value conflicts, or other frictions or needs for creativity, vision, and change in their workplace. The director can listen in prayer for how they may be called to respond, if at all, to the directee's proposed action. Some of the kinds of questions that have occurred to me include such things as:

1. How specifically are they listening for and noticing God's hand in the situation?
2. Where are their fears and hopes that can be offered to God?
3. Where might their support come from beyond their own prayerfulness?

The director's ongoing prayer and care for the person is one form of support that can encourage a person to go forward with a risky or time-consuming sense of calling. Support for directees' presence for God in the workplace in general as well as in such specific difficult situations can be important. A director might ask whether there is anyone else in the workplace who shares their spiritual sensitivity. If so, can they be in mutual prayer for each other? Can they perhaps meet periodically for prayer and reflect on how they are being present for God in the workplace? Are they sensing any mutual calling related to the organization's life where they can collaborate? If there is no such person who surfaces in the workplace, perhaps there are friends or church members who would be interested in being mutually supportive for prayerfulness.

One potential contemplative offering to the workplace is recognition of the value of a listening, spacious silence that challenges the sense of driven human autonomy that can easily dominate the workplace. There is something about an open silence that can free God's Presence and guidance to appear and egos to diminish, even when that intent isn't clearly in people's minds during the silence. If such silence is part of a directee's spiritual life, they may find themselves probing a potential call to suggest that silence for others in the workplace. If the organization is explicitly religiously grounded, this silence can be suggested with an explicitly spiritual intent. Suggestions, as they may seem called for, can include such things as:

1. Setting aside brief periods of collective, nonworking silence for prayer, with the participants either gathered together or in place at their workstations, with the beginning and ending of this time signaled by a bell;

2. Setting aside a certain part of the day, week, or month when work is done as much as possible in silence, with the intent of practicing the Presence in an especially mindful way that hopefully can carry over into other times;

3. Including planned times of silence in meetings—at the beginning and perhaps at the end as well, and in-between, whenever someone may call for it—all with the intent of letting what happens be cocreated with God rather than being seen as an autonomous human work.

In secular organizations I have heard amazing stories of receptivity to silence, especially in the context of meetings, though the spiritual intent usually cannot be up-front in suggesting it (however, this is beginning to change as interest in spirituality in the workplace has greatly increased in recent years). The wording of the motivation for having silence needs to be adapted to the particular work context. It might include something about giving people space to listen for what they really need to do, space to get beneath the surface busyness, tiredness, and drivenness, or space for creative reflection. A brief silence can also be suggested as a norm whenever a meeting becomes hung-up or overly intense, as a way to settle down and "let in" an openness to what is best for the group.

Directees who are really practicing the Presence in the workplace may find themselves unintentionally radiating a quality of presence that is picked up by other people in the office or other work setting. This might include someone whom the Spirit is bringing to the directee for mutual spiritual support in the workplace. It may also be someone who is at a particularly open, searching place in life, someone whom God's Spirit is moving in a particularly strong way. Such an individual may be drawn to the directee as someone they sense can be helpful to them in sorting out what is going on and what is called for.

Directees may find themselves in the position of becoming informal spiritual companions for such people. This can be a privileged relationship that is one of the fruits of the directee's ongoing desire to be given to God in the workplace. It can be more difficult if the two people are in a subordinate or superior role relationship in the work setting; in such a case the spiritual relationship may need to be kept carefully bracketed from the actual practical work relationship so that it can be as honest and free of the work role as possible. It may develop that the directee will need to refer such a person to someone else for a long-term spiritual direction relationship.

The director can be theologically sensitive to the place of work in human life. In the Bible and in Judeo-Christian tradition a rhythm of work and rest time (or ministry and Sabbath time) is prescribed, as I briefly mentioned in chapter four. Beyond the practical reality of our need for rest lies a deeper theological truth: we are created as unconditionally loved beings, created for an end-in-itself love affair with the One who gives life. Work at its best is meant to be an overflow of this love affair, not a means of ultimately justifying our existence and earning divine love. We exist for more than work.

The call to Sabbath time above all is the call to give space for an end-in-itself appreciation of life in God and to let this overflow into a God-centered work life. Our dignity rests in our trust that we are loved before, through, and beyond our works. This view clashes with a cultural view that often values life only in terms of its productivity. Directees can be tempted to ignore their calling to nonproductive time, when they can just appreciate the divine Presence, creation, and themselves as end-in-themselves gifts of love. Such Sabbath time can take many forms, such as walks in the woods, sitting before something beautiful, play, anything that for the directee invites an appreciation of life just as it is. When directees are seen to be driven to fill all their time with work when there is no economic necessity to do so, the director may be moved to question how God has been understood and invited into their lives.

If directees are unemployed or retired, then they may be especially in need of remembering their value in God's eyes apart from their work, especially in a culture where a person's value is closely connected to work. Such people, detached from their normal work routines, also may find themselves newly questioning God's nature and involvement with them. It can be a particularly vulnerable and disorienting time in which the director might play a vital part in helping them to probe more deeply the currents of the Spirit in their lives.

Cultures tend to value certain kinds of work much more than other kinds. Directees can find themselves tempted to join the culture's view and lose the spiritual perspective that values all kinds of work that provide true service to God's creation as equal sacramental arenas of grace, no matter how humble the work may be in the culture's eyes. Often directees are involved in "tent-making" ministries, like St. Paul, which they do not consider their deepest callings but which keep bread on the table. The deepest calling may be to kinds of work that could never support them, if they pay anything at all, such as many kinds of volunteer religious and social service and family care.

Sometimes directors may be called upon to be part of their directees' discernment as to whether or not to quit their jobs and follow their heart sense of what is life-giving and valuable to them and others, but which would involve much less income and perhaps the disapproval of others. Directors can be particularly helpful as people with whom directees can test such leanings before God and find support for whatever may show itself as true soul-callings.

In general, the direction relationship can symbolize an alternative value system to the often illusory sirens and ways of the culture in the workplace that miss their divine center. Spiritual direction as described in this book is forever holding up the centrality of our turning to the liberating and immediate divine Presence in all of our discernment and action, in and out of the workplace.[5]

Spiritual Community — *over denominational rifts?*

Embracing divine love as the heart of our own loves is not easy, given both the mysterious subtlety of its presence and the temptation to substitute more ego-securing loves. As we struggle with the discernments and willingness involved in embracing God, we realize our need for practical spiritual community. We often seek an intentional covenanting with a group of people who share our conscious desire for the truth and love of God and of God's vision for the world, and who share our long-term willingness to let go that which would turn us away from this loving truth. We also need a community willing to be patient enough with our resistances along the way and willing to give inviting room for the Spirit to expand our active loving.

Many directees will bring with them a dream for true spiritual community. Usually it is an elusive dream. It is not often found in the household community as we would like. The local church provides a skeleton for such a vision and is sometimes graced with the realization of truly God-grounded spiritual community. There seems to be a growing hunger for such an ideal grounding in churches. Often, however, the congregation's life is caught up in narrower human-grounded community and outreach efforts that, regardless of all their well-intentioned purposes, are not approached in ways that adequately support our sense of immediate belonging to and givenness to God. Perhaps something of this might also ring true with some vowed religious communities of sisters and brothers. Scripture and church history can be seen as a long story of the elusive and transient nature of true spiritual community, depicting a human yearning for it that will not be finally satisfied with less.

In attending this dimension of a directee's spiritual life, it can be helpful to remember that spiritual community exists not only in an intentionally gathered group of people. It also exists in any communal setting at those times when we find ourselves heeding the always present Spirit of God that would weave liberating, loving truth through the tapestry of our relationships.

At its purest, these experiences of spiritual community can involve such spontaneous, direct attunement to the living Spirit in the moment that we are not aware of anything special happening. We spontaneously put our arm around someone grieving, an act that may open that person to a larger divine caring. We say something without premeditation that is gently funny and frees a larger, connecting truth to lighten an ego-heavy atmosphere. We allow together an experience of deeply accepting, collective unity that reveals our larger unity in God.

Our lives are full of such moments of spiritual community. These times reflect the truth that such community exists not by human engineering, but by the living Spirit revealing the community that is always present in God and always being reverberated in some way. The whole creation can be called God's pulsing, interconnected community, the great Body of Christ in its fullest, realized sense. At any given moment, we can visibly share certain manifestations of this community. It is always a potential reality right where we are at a given time. Spiritual community is not elsewhere. It is always waiting to be uncovered right here, right now.

Given the great fragmentation of our consciousness and identities in most of the communal contexts we find ourselves, however, it is difficult to sustain this awareness of spiritual community. We naturally yearn for a group of people who can support our yearning and willingness for such community in a fuller and enduring way. The spiritual direction relationship itself is an arena of communal support. Meeting once a month with someone is not sufficiently sustaining for many people, however. If it doesn't already exist for the directee, the director may be called to encourage the directee to form or join a small group of people who are dedicated to a deep and authentic spiritual life together. Such a group can pray and reflect on the spiritual journey and any called-for actions, grounded in the deep soul-identity that forms the seedbed of spiritual community.

Following are some questions that may help to sensitize the director to the ballpark of spiritual community, and you may think of others. If this area of a directee's life shows itself as one where the Spirit seems to be moving at a given time, then the director and directee need to lean back into the spacious Presence and listen for what is given. The really important questions and probing responses will be given spontaneously on the spot, as these may be heard.

1. Who besides the spiritual director are the people and groups that now support the directee in their spiritual lives, if any?

2. What are some recent moments of spiritual community in directees' lives where God's Spirit has been apparent?

3. Given what they have found to be Spirit-conveying and Spirit-denying in their lives with other people and how their own spiritual lives and callings are evolving at this point, what kind of intentional spiritual community might they be drawn to now? (I.e., what do they want to gather with others for? And with whom, when, with what commitment?) Can they find such a group in their local church (or do they see the whole congregation as such a community)? Do they need some other spiritual center—among their family, friends, neighbors, or coworkers?

4. If they already belong to such a community, is there anything that they now prayerfully sense needs to be given attention personally or as a community that might help it to become a more honest and true supporter of God's living Spirit personally and in the world?

LITURGICAL PRAYER

Spiritual community finds its corporate heart in times of common prayer. The very gathering together in desire for the Real One proclaimed by Jesus brings the fulfillment of his promise, often repeated in this book, that wherever two or three gather in his name, his living Spirit will be among them. In this sense a silent Quaker meeting can express the basic sacramental quality of corporate worship just as much as the Eucharist does in many other traditions. The spiritual direction session itself can be seen as a liturgical act: two (or more) people gathering with the desire for God, invoking God's presence in prayer and reflecting on their living personal story of grace in relation to the larger story of grace carried by the communal tradition.

Experience of the formal corporate tradition of liturgical prayer in the background of directees will likely have been significantly formative of their experience and interpretation of divine presence, consciously or unconsciously. A formal Eucharist, for example, the historic heart of most corporate Christian worship, has a way of being an ongoing school for spiritual formation. All our faculties are potentially opened to the divine on many levels, from the primal emotional to the refined aesthetic. Individual and corporate dimensions of experience come together, extending through an integrated sense of time: past, present, and future, and beyond time into God's eternal now. The Eucharist invites a turning from self to God in community. Affective relations with others are often acutely sharpened, heightening an awareness of community in God and with others. Where images of our connection with the rest of divine creation are included, we are shown our larger community and interdependence with all living beings on the earth and with the cosmos beyond.

The physical exchange of peace or handshake encourages reconciliation. The words of liturgy help to interpret and guide our experience. The dialectic revealed between God and persons in the words of liturgy and in the sermon teach listening and response to callings. The collection expresses a shared community of goods. Praising teaches us praise. Confession manifests responsibility and forgiveness. The celebrative quality shows forth the end-in-itself quality of life in God's love and the goodness of God. The liturgical year, where used, makes visible the full drama of salvation history, and where particular saints are included, it raises up models of holiness, particularly when the list is expanded to include informal saints among us—such people in their great diversity become reminders of the universal call to holiness. In the bread and wine we see that the material and spiritual, as well as life and death, are shown together as one interwoven and redeemed reality in Christ.

Such formative qualities of the Eucharist can be particularly helpful in challenging many social and spiritual distortions of grace and reality. For example, they counter a private, nonhistorical sense of God that does not adequately show our integral connection with others in the past, present, and future. They also challenge a vengeful and violent rather than a forgiving and peace-seeking response to individual and communal problems in the light of the divine sacrifice. Such examples point to the Eucharist as counter-cultural, putting into perspective and challenging many of the values and forces in and around us.[6]

Of course, the Eucharist and other formal corporate worship forms can be negatively formative as well as positively formative of the spiritual life. We see this where they effectively deny some of the gospel qualities reflected above. Most directees bring a mixed history of positive and negative formation in formal common prayer from their experience. Their own ongoing personal spiritual experience will sometimes find context and guidance from that setting. At other times it may result in their feeling alienated or confused in corporate worship. The more direct awareness and desire one has for God, the more difficult it can be to gather with people many of whom the directee feels do not share, and indeed fear, such experience and deep spiritual motivation. This difficulty can be compounded when there are major personality conflicts with the leaders and/or others present. "Going to church" may be a great struggle for such people, a struggle that they bring to the direction relationship for discernment, just as they might bring the difficulty of living with others who are in a different place spiritually.

Directees may be called to a simple faithfulness in such situations, trusting that God is at work with others in

God's own different way and that no corporate prayer form can meet the particular personal needs of all its participants at a given time. They may be called instead to withdraw from participation in a particular church and seek another one, or to give weight to more informal gatherings of highly motivated seekers of God.

Given the sacramental quality of gathering for God in some form, with all the perspective, mutual challenge and support it can offer to each other's spiritual awareness and action, it could be a great loss to the directee's spiritual life to be cut off completely from any liturgical gathering for a long period. The person's absence would be a loss to the spiritual community as well. Our core spiritual community is with God, but the very communal triune nature of God in Christian tradition invites us to gather and be refreshed with others who appreciate God's presence and yearn for the fullness of God's shalom in creation. Without such authentic gatherings we are more prone to forget our common calling and to fall into the world's or our own personal illusions and isolation.

Following are three questions that might help you personally reflect on the relation of corporate worship/liturgy to your spiritual life and to the spiritual life of your directees as this area may show itself in a direction session. Again, I am not suggesting that these particular questions be asked of a directee but that they help sensitize you to ways liturgy/corporate worship is connected to the spiritual life.

1. How has your experience of liturgy/corporate worship awakened and sustained your sense of the divine and of the corporate spiritual life?

2. How has your spiritual life outside of corporate worship led you to bring a greater sense of receptivity to God? How has it made it more difficult to participate in liturgy/corporate worship?

3. What kind of liturgy/corporate worship do you feel most assists your presence for God and for an awareness of the world in God at this point, and where do or might you find such a gathering?

Cultural Pluralism

Culture is a human-constructed sea in which we swim. It refers to those shared social structures, values, places, languages, and practices that form both an unconscious and conscious orientation to reality. It is the necessary colored lens through which we see life, except at the most direct level of knowing. It is particularly complex when we take into consideration ethnic, religious, regional, and other subcultures within a larger shared culture.

Culture is shaped by our shared desires and fears in the face of life's many impinging forces. It is spiritually ambiguous. Sometimes it supports transparency for God. Sometimes it supports idolatry: a displacement of God by a variety of finite images that have become ultimate definers and securers of reality for us. Culture thus needs to be approached with discernment rather than with blanket affirmation or rejection.

Apophatic spiritual tradition can be a vital aid in approaching culture without idolatry of its images, because it puts such weight on relativizing our images to that which is beyond their grasp. It is awareness of the transcendence of God, for example, that frees us when we are praying with a classical icon not to worship the image of wood and paint. God can be present for us in the image, but God is not confined to the image. As I implied earlier in this book, the image can be a sacramental vehicle through which God's radiant presence can be revealed to us, but it does not contain the fullness of God nor is it an exclusive conveyor or definer of God. And so it is with all our images, inside and outside of our minds.

We may have a directee who belongs to a particular series of cultural or subcultural groups, say a sixty-year-old African American United Methodist homemaker in a Chicago middle-class family and neighborhood. Consciously or unconsciously, our minds may have a particular set of stereotypical images of the directee based on this description, and the directee may share the same or related self-images. These images may have a certain ultimate, unshakable quality about them in our minds. Then we are in particular danger of letting the images dominate the way we hear that person. We lose our freedom to let the directee be the unique person of God's creation that he or she is. Culture certainly is part of our conditioned identity, and God can be at work in that conditioning, but it does not define our souls, which are always more than our cultural accretions.

The more spiritually aware we become, that is, the more sensitive to the inclusive and liberating nature of divine love, the more likely we are to come into conflict with a culture's many exclusive loves. The refusal to give ultimate "authority" to particular racial, ethnic, or class values, or to particular political or culturally defined moral values can be very threatening to people whose identity and security are wrapped up in such qualities. It is no accident that spiritual martyrdom, in the sense of dying as a witness to the larger loving truth, is seen so much in human history, of which Jesus' martyrdom is the deep exemplar. His death particularly reveals God's involvement with us in this witness.

Our deep spiritual calling is to let grace secure us in God beyond the security of the culture. Indeed, we are called to be secured in God even beyond the subculture of the church, even beyond any particular image of God, secured finally only in a naked trust of the One who *is,* beyond all our naming. That kind of security is what gives us the freedom to be with ourselves and our directees in ways that are not defined and confined by the womb of the culture. Then the culture, like our ego, is free to be an expediently functional and even playful vehicle of our larger identity in God.

When we are with a directee who shares most of our cultural and subcultural values and general experience, we need to be alert to how we may share certain blind spots. For example, in much of middle-class North American culture (as in many others) it is difficult to talk about how much money we have, how we spend it, and what it means to us. Money is often considered a very private area. We do not easily bring to prayer or to other people our feelings about having it, spending it, and understanding it as an icon or idol, despite all the time Jesus spends talking about money (especially in Luke's Gospel). As a result, we might tacitly agree with the directee that probing questions about money in relation to God are off-limits, ignoring the fact that money is an arena of great power in most people's lives. We then lose the freedom to open this difficult arena to God's grace even though the Spirit may be inviting us to do so together.[7]

When we are with a directee from a different culture than ours, our knowledge and ability to "live into" their cultural differences and overlaps can be important if we are to understand what they are saying about their experience in relation to God. For example, people from certain cultures can greatly value harmony in human relationships, sometimes to the point of publicly denying any felt disharmony. If you asked such a directee how he or she felt about your direction relationship, their cultural conditioning might lead them to say that everything is fine, when in fact it may not be. You would need to probe further to uncover what is really going on.

Another example can be seen in those cultures where there is no or little sense of self-identity apart from a communal, cultural one. If the director of such a person assumes that individual rights and private needs always take priority over the needs of that person's cultural community, they will be expressing an individualistic cultural bias that may not always be attuned to God's way for this person. On the other hand, the director might be so blindly affirming of the directee's cultural values that they do not notice or support the directee's valid sense of invitation by the Spirit to something countercultural, that may risk censure from others.

Too much attention to cultural differences, however, can become counterproductive. A director once spoke of trying too hard to understand a directee who was very different culturally. Her extreme effort itself became a distraction from her presence to God and put too much weight on seeking more accurate images of the person. She discovered that it was more important to lean openly into God, giving room for the mystery of God's Spirit to show itself in its own surprising ways both through and beyond cultural boundaries. That graced process is always more than our cultural or personal understanding can comprehend. "God's Word," as we read in 2 Timothy 2:9, "is not bound," including not being bound by any particular culture or set understanding. God has in mind for us more than we can possibly imagine, more than we can "image" (Eph 3:20).[8]

Following is an exercise that might help sensitize you to the influence of culture in yourself and your direction relationships. More particularly, it might help you notice the possible idolatry and transparency to God that can exist in our cultural overlaps and differences. It might also help you notice some particular spontaneous, culture-transcending times of innocent presence.

1. Think of a directee who is most different from you cultur- ally. In two parallel columns, describe some of your own and that person's cultural characteristics (for example: ethnic group, faith tradition, class, race, age group, education, dress, urban/rural background, geographical region where raised, language, type of work, etc.).

2. Look over the two columns: how is your attentiveness to God for the person, and sense of her/his uniqueness, affected by the similarities and differences, especially by the weight, the ultimacy that you give to them?

3. Give an example, if you can, of:

    a. how you have been limited in the direction relation- ship by your cultural context;

    b. how the cultural context has been sacramental for the directee, that is, how grace has shone through it;

    c. a spontaneous, culture-transcending time of innocent presence, a time unmediated by culture; a time of spon- taneous awareness, connectedness, which was appar- ent before your interpretive (and therefore culturally influenced) level of knowing became operational. If nothing comes to mind, you might imagine yourself simply looking into the eyes of your directee with no mental images of the person, just a spacious, open sense of connectedness with their unique soul in God.

NON-CHRISTIAN SPIRITUAL TRADITIONS

One special dimension of pluralism in spiritual direction concerns non-Christian spiritual traditions. Probably most spiritual directors and their directees today have some expe- rience of one or more such traditions. It may be as brief as a little story or saying, heard or read somewhere. It may be as extensive as having spent time studying, praying with, and perhaps even belonging to another tradition. At no time in the past have so many of the writings of great spiritual fig- ures in other traditions been available in English (or for that matter of great spiritual figures in earlier Christian tradition). With immigrants to North America and other English-speaking areas coming from an increasingly wide range of religious backgrounds, together with local converts to these traditions, many other religions are increasingly alive in our communities. Educational systems increasingly take this pluralism into account, so that at least a superficial knowledge of other traditions is increasing.[9]

What is the impact of this growing encounter with the world's deep spiritual traditions on ourselves and our directees? There is a continuum of possible responses. At one extreme, where there are high boundaries and a need to cling to what one knows, there may also be hostility, rejection, and even a pattern of ignoring other traditions. In the middle, there may be a selective interest, seen in our use of some saying or practice from another tradition that we have found helpful to our own prayer and understanding. At the other end, many things about another tradition may be more spiritually enlivening than anything in one's own tradition at the moment, and we may even be considering a commitment to that other tradition.

We need to ask ourselves how much we believe that God's Spirit wants to show itself to us in another tradition. We do not need to be clear about what God may have in mind about any long-term reconciliation of different traditions. We do not have to have an intimate knowledge of the history and schools of spirituality in any given tradition. But we do need to be in touch with our own sense of openness and closedness to what may come to us at a given time from another tradition. Is it irrelevant to us? Is it something about which we need to be very careful and suspicious? Do we perceive it as a threat to our accustomed, conditioned way of approaching the divine?

Do we feel we have all we can deal with and need in an explicitly Christian tradition, even if there may be something of validity in other traditions? Do we feel particularly drawn to the freshness of something in another tradition at this point? Do we sense we will find a deeper perspective of our own tradition through visiting another one? Whatever our views as directors, what is likely to be their effect on the way we listen to directees telling us about their experiences within other traditions?

When we speak of a spiritual tradition we need to remember that it is not a static, simple affair. All deep spiritual traditions, as living systems of long duration, are very complex, dynamic entities that often overlap one another. The label of a spiritual tradition covers a vast spectrum of experiences, behaviors, attitudes, interpretations, practices, and sources of knowledge. Together these form a certain patterned way of seeing and living life. The pattern, however, can hold many tensions within it, as we see in the historically different strands of Christian tradition and in different stages of the spiritual life.

Because we are involved with the living Spirit of God and our own living spirits, there is a dynamic quality to the spiritual heart of a tradition. We see the often surprising fruits of the ongoing divine-human encounter in the historical biographies of individuals and groups. These fruits in time can affect the self-understanding and practices of the larger tradition of which they are a part, even as the tradition may hold to certain constants. God seems to keep shaking the kaleidoscope of human living within a particular tradition, thereby keeping us on our spiritual toes.

Christian tradition, like others, is a dynamic tradition dating back to its Hebrew roots, when Abraham and Sarah were called to venture forth from their settled environment at Ur in Chaldea to a new and unknown land in trust that the "more" God had in mind for them was for the best. The expansive Spirit of God in so much of scripture and church history seems to beckon us beyond our tribal and sectarian securities in order to settle new terrains of the Spirit, as we are drawn by God toward a fully "catholic" faith, that is, a faith as fully inclusive of God's truth as possible.

There is always growing room for us in this quest. In a sense, only God is fully catholic, but God is forever stretching us toward a greater fullness of the divine loving truth. Perhaps Christians cannot say they have a fully universal religion, despite the fullness of the Gospel, until they recognize the largeness of Christ, the one who said, "...before Abraham was, I am" (John 8:58), the one who, as St. Paul says, fills the whole creation (Eph 1:23). In this big sense of Christ, he is not the monopoly of Christians. He is not only Jesus of Nazareth, as the theologian Raimon Pannikar has pointed out. The Spirit of God that is in Christ can be seen to be generously present throughout the world. That Spirit connects us to the truth wherever it is.

Such a view reflects and extends the growing positive nature of interfaith dialogue and prayer that has been fostered in the last few decades in many mainstream Christian traditions. The Second Vatican Council's document on non-Christian religions speaks for this newly open view when it states that Roman Catholics are to "acknowledge, preserve, and promote the spiritual and moral goods of other religions, rejecting nothing that is true and holy in them." Christian tradition in this open stance is seen as witnessing to God in Christ for the world as we trust and have experienced that reality, and listening, learning, and exploring with those touched by the divine in different ways.

In an interdependent world desperately in need of unity grounded in the gracious trust of divine Presence, we can collaborate with others in our overlaps, our common ground, desiring to find signs of God's graciousness in other traditions as well as in our own. We can also value our differences as opportunities to illuminate our blind spots and to go deeper in our understanding of the divine truth carried by our own tradition.

With this view, spiritual directors would lean toward a discerning openness when faced with a directee's experience of the divine through something found under the heading of a different tradition, just as they would in hearing of any other experience. It might be helpful for the director to remember that there is an almost universal witness in all deep world religions to three major values relevant to the spiritual life:

1. The value of having a spiritual guide who embodies and carries the spirit of the tradition.

2. The value of obedience to a disciplined path, at least in the early stages of all traditions, leading toward an inner realization of the tradition's truth and a personal identity with the divine at the center of one's being. In each tradition we find the spread of classical paths mentioned in chapter four, especially devotion, action, and knowledge, which at their best are seen as complementary to one another.

3. An ultimate goal and hope of individual and collective liberation from the confines of the little self, that sense of identity that is ego-centered, with its concomitant anxious, willful, ignorant, confused, narrowed-away-from-God orientation. The liberation itself is marked by an embodied "wise loving," a quality of selfless wisdom and compassion, of light and love, that reflects the nature of the divine in us.

Where we sense the compatibility of ultimate purpose in another tradition with that of our own, we can more easily find ourselves open to use certain words and practices from that tradition that enhance our way to the truth of God without sacrifice to Christian truth. Such a visit to another tradition can bring us back to our own with a more subtle and profound sense of the truth it is trying to convey. What makes any form Christian, I believe, is its intent, not its particular form. If our intent is deepening vulnerability to the Spirit of Christ in us, then any form that we find helping us to foster that will be compatible. Christian tradition, including scripture, is full of words and forms borrowed from non-Christian sources. These are taken up because they are able to further the truth of God revealed in Christ.

As we may have our eyes opened to the larger world's spiritual experience, though, I think we need to be careful not to support digging shallow holes in every spiritual tradition, expecting to hit groundwater, as tempting as that is in a time when so much is available to us. Those of us who have found the larger loving truth of life in the Christian way are called to realize and offer God through the unique ways God's face is shown for the world in this tradition. The deeper we find ourselves in Christ, however, the more likely we are to recognize spiritual truth (and untruth) wherever we encounter it, both in and out of our own tradition.

If we find a directee moved to take up any learning or practice from another deep spiritual tradition, some questions we might have in our own mind are these:

1. How does their involvement grow out of and feed into their prayer?
2. How is it affecting their relationship to the divine?
3. What are its fruit, especially in terms of their consonance with the fruit of the Spirit as named in scripture (Gal 5:22ff.)?

I have restricted myself to speaking of well-established and long-tested world religious traditions. If a directee is involved with a new or eclectic religious group, though, these same questions would apply. An involvement about which I think we should raise very serious questions from the start, however, would be with a Satanic cult, given the universally negative experience I have heard from people so involved. However, it is unlikely such a person would ever be in spiritual direction with a Christian, Jew, or anyone else committed to a mainstream world religious tradition, unless they were trying to pull away from such an involvement.

Social Vision •

Some years ago a priest I know was jailed by what was then a very oppressive regime in Bolivia for his social/political activities. The Bible he had brought with him was confiscated as subversive literature. The regime was rightly aware and afraid of the powerful divine sanction given in scripture to justice seeking and the larger scriptural vision of which justice seeking is a part: a vision of a God-centered, humane, and shalom-seeking society.

Jesus' intimacy with God had implications for human community, as was true before him with Moses and the Hebrew prophets. Out of that intimacy grows a social vision of the reign of God rising among us, for which we pray repeatedly in the Lord's Prayer. This reign that will bring into being the full commonwealth of God is based on a self-emptying love radiating between God and God's creation. The Spirit has a place for everyone as a vessel of this God-inspired communal love. Spiritual direction takes place in the context of this inclusive social vision.

We find many specific signs of God's kindom in the Gospels: in the Beatitudes; in the poor having good news preached to them; when the blind see, the deaf hear, the lame walk; when the marginalized are included in our community and are seen as channels of the Spirit for us as well as for themselves. God's reign is also seen when we appreciate beauty and goodness; when the value of riches is seen in their instrumentality for God's shalom; and when we see the wealth of our personal gifts as servants of that shalom as well. We see God's reign also when mercy tempers justice with eyes that see each situation in its uniqueness and in the context of God's love for what God has created, even when we stray.

We are called to join this way of God and cocreate its forms with God's empowering and leading Spirit. The fullness of God's shalom is yet to be revealed and its timing is in God's hands. It is a fullness that includes an affirmation of whatever is of God in our common and personal histories, histories that to faith are hallowed by God's Incarnation among us.

That fullness will stretch beyond what is possible in social structures and roles, as we see expressed in the practice of historic sabbath time. During that special time we are called to live in a quality of shared community that lightens and even collapses social categories, in anticipation of the heavenly sabbath without end. But in the normal daily social conditions in which God allows us to live, social structures and role relationships in the family, work, church, and politics are necessary for most human collective life. As long as this is true, just social structures with mutually respectful and serving roles are constitutive of God's way among us. Attention to our calling in this area thus is a constitutive dimension of the spiritual life.

Since the fullness of history is beyond our human understanding, much less our control, we need to retain a certain humility before the mystery of God's ways. Any social-political ideology must be relative to this divine mystery, constantly exposed to God in prayer for purification. We all are involved in some ideology that provides us with the mental structure we need in order to have and carry out any social vision. That mental structure will include a series of assumptions about what is socially valuable and what is needed to live out and spread those values. But ideology, in a Christian context, is a provisional, open construct that needs to be kept open to God's ongoing leading. This need not reduce the energy and commitment needed to effectively follow a given social view, but it prevents us from identifying with the view so completely that it becomes a securing substitute for, rather than provisional instrument of, God's ever-evolving leadership.

In a nation like the United States the church's (and other major religious bodies') social vision becomes particularly important, because there is presently so little held up as a positive vision on a major national scale. Great weight is given to "negative" freedoms: freedom "froms" that leave the individual or separate special-interest groups at the center of things, with little that transcends their self-interests and little that helps us to have a common sense of mutually caring and inclusive life together. The church at its best offers a vision of freedom "for" something, for a transcendent covenant that unites us all, and all of creation with us, in God. In scripture the covenant with Noah handed down after the flood perhaps best reflects an inclusive covenant. At its best the church is always calling people both through and beyond self-preoccupation, family identity, nationalism, ethnicity, commercialism, and social oppression to a larger and more given-to-God vision.

Today we have an ever-widening sense of global context for social discernment. We are all novices at global envisioning and responsibility. We are novices at looking for *social* as well as individual consolation and desolation (to use Ignatian terminology). In spiritual direction, for example, we may need to look at the impact on our prayer and relation to God of a *social* sense of desolation that we are experiencing, such as a sense of helplessness in the face of some oppressive political situation. We can also notice the impact of a social sense of consolation, such as a sense of empowerment to help alleviate a particular socially oppressive situation with community support. Direction includes an opportunity, as it may be given, to listen in prayer together for how the directee may be called in the social arena, in terms of a call to prayer and a call to action.

Directees may be called to join God's prayer for many social situations, but they cannot realistically respond beyond intercessory prayer to everything encountered. Mass media, beyond our own direct experiences, places countless situations of social need before us, leaving us in danger of becoming numbed and paralyzed beyond a moment of prayer. In direction we can listen together for perhaps one or two real calls to action for which a person may feel genuine energy, capacity, and peace at this point in his or her life. This may be something very simple and easy, or it may be something much more demanding and risky, perhaps something that needs discernment over a period of time. The director can listen for signals of social vision and concern, as well as for resistances, in whatever directees bring to sessions. When such things show themselves, the director might note:

1. *Are they brought to prayer?*
2. *Do they ask what God would have them pray for in the social arena?*

At the right moment the director might help a person to articulate the dream God is dreaming in them of some dimension of God's shalom and the place of their gifts in its realization. Sometimes a person cannot act on a call without its being a shared call, as when a refugee family may need sponsoring and a number of people are needed to share the costs and care, or when there is a call to make health care more accessible to the poor in a city and many others are needed to launch an effective effort. The director, if so moved, can remind a person of the possibility of such a collective call.

In the process of listening to directees speak of their callings in the social arena, directors sometimes may find *themselves* being reached by God through the directees, as they sense an invitation (and maybe resistance) to some particular kind of prayer, envisioning, and action in their own lives.

Some called-for social actions will risk conflict, personal resources, and even life itself. Prayer can be offered to see, act, and suffer if necessary, out of a sense of God's empowered love rather than out of fear or hate. The director can be a helpful and prayerful presence in helping to test and sustain a person through such difficult calls, including during times when directees sense the failure of envisioned results in their efforts. In such times, beyond sharing the person's grief, the director can invite a person to turn more deeply to God, in trust that their efforts are received with the love with which they were given and that God is still involved, capable of redeeming any situation in God's own way and time. In all dimensions of social envisioning, as in all other aspects of the directee's life, I believe that the director's most steady encouragement needs to be for the directee's desire for ongoing immediate presence for God through whatever is happening, in their prayer and in their actions.

Here are a few further questions that might be helpful in sensitizing you to the social/political context of the spiritual life:[10]

1. Can you recall an incident where you sensed an encounter with God's Spirit through your involvement in the social-political arena?

2. How was this nourished by your prayer life?

3. How was your prayer fed by your encounter with the Spirit in the social-political arena?

4. Do your directees (and you) expect that embracing God has social-political consequences? Have you heard any possible indications of calling in the social-political arena? Do you sense anything in your own hopes, fears, or confusions in this area that may hinder your openness to God for your directees as they speak about this area of their lives? If so, have you opened these to God in prayer?

5. Does your life as you live it seem to be a validation of your prayer as you pray it?

Among All God's Creatures •

We are new at ecological envisioning and responsibility today, just as we are at global social awareness. In our over-separation from nature, which is driven by a vision of domination, human material comfort, and commercial profit, enabled by our technological capacity to reshape the earth, we have exploited the living ecosystem of the planet to the point of threat to its long-term capacity to sustain itself. We have not loved our neighbor as ourselves, in this case, the neighbors that are our fellow creatures on the earth. That love and sense of mutual belonging needs to be genuine, not just a matter of guilt, if the depth of caring that is needed is to be sustained.

A great deal of recent theological reflection has reminded us that, though humans have a special place in creation, we nonetheless are an integral part of it. Our very bodies are made of the same matter as the stars. All material life can be seen metaphorically as the skin of God's Body. Our minds and habits share a great deal of overlap with other creatures. We have the capacity not only to exploit them for our ends, but to appreciate and care for them as part of our stewardship of God's living forms among us and to learn from them about God. Eastern Orthodox tradition emphasizes the permeation of creation with God's uncreated energies. With that understanding we could say that the physical world is iconic: everything in it is capable of showing us something of God, and something of our own nature and community.

In addition to relooking at Christian sources, we can look to other traditions to help us in understanding our stewardship and relationship with nature. Buddhist tradition, for example, includes regular prayers for all sentient beings (and some scientists speculate that even rocks have feelings!). In Mahayana Buddhist tradition, a great saint will vow not to go to heaven, to final nirvana, until all sentient beings are saved. The reincarnational view of that tradition would have you look at a bird or another creature in your path as a potential reincarnation of a deceased parent or other close relation, and thus to be cared for and reverenced. In Tibet, where a normal Buddhist vegetarian diet was difficult due to the altitude and terrain, if you were forced to kill an animal for food, you would do so with respect and ask forgiveness of the animal.

One of the grounds of renewed interest in Native American religions is that in them, as in other nonliterate traditions around the world that have remained closely tied to nature for survival and understanding, there is much respect shown for the living quality of the earth and sky we share. Such traditions teach us what we have lost in urbanized societies: that our "spiritual community" stretches to include all that God has created.

There is a difficult side to nature for us. It is a mystery that there are dangerous animals to avoid or kill. (It is interesting to note, however, that certain great saints in various traditions are reputed to have lived peacefully even with these. We also see that the vision in Isaiah 11 of life "filled with the knowledge of God" includes the elimination of harm between humans and animals.) Beyond animals, it is a mystery why there are so many deadly bacteria and viruses. Physical death itself is a great mystery, despite all the theological attempts to explain it. There is a tenuous quality to this plane of existence.

Human life, at the very least, requires the sacrifice of plants to sustain itself, if not necessarily the death of animals. But there can be a humble and respectful acceptance of limits to this destruction. As I see it, we can maintain a view of no unnecessary killing, and we can accept the limitation of our lifespans without the idolatry of trying to sustain them beyond their time at the expense of other life. We can be willing to die trusting God and in love with God's creation, just as we can be willing to live in such trust and love.

One way God connects us with nature is through giving us the capacity to appreciate and be fascinated by its beauty. We find nature marked by such patterns as simplicity, harmony, balance, and a mysterious quality of vibrancy. When we want a place to retreat, we will often choose a place of natural beauty. We instinctively sense that God will somehow come through that environment for us and show us something we need to see and embrace in our own nature.

As with human culture, nature is ambiguous, but it is part of our larger body (and we are a part of its body); it can be a sacrament of divine Presence. "Consider the lilies of the field..."(Matt 6:28).

This spiritual ecological understanding opens two relevant avenues of human calling for spiritual directors to be aware of as their directees spontaneously reflect on nature from time to time:

1. The first has to do with *appreciation.* You may notice your directees showing a variety of forms of appreciation of nature over time. They may mention signs of God's Presence in nature. They may mention particular manifestations of nature that draw them closer to that Presence—whether in the backyard, or with pets, or in the woods, mountains, rivers, oceans, deserts, parks, or gazing through a telescope. They may speak of the fruit of that sense of Presence (such as some special guidance or sense of healing that has been given them) and how it leaves them feeling about spiritual companionship with other creatures. They may also speak of how the pressures of their lives have dulled their appreciation of this larger community of God.

2. The second area of calling has to do with *action.* Directees may sense in their prayer one or more particular callings to participate in the care of the earth. This might involve anything from gardening to particular conservation efforts to involvement with an environmental organization to starting a reflection group at church or in some other learning environment. If they sense a loss of connectedness, they may need to be encouraged to ask God what it is in the pressures or other circumstances of their lives that is distancing them from the rest of nature and how God may want to empower them to reconnect again in some way.[11]

The Creature of Our Human Body

Implicitly, there is also a third area of ecological concern: appreciating and caring for our own physical bodies. Our bodies form an ecological subsystem in themselves.

They are temples of God's Spirit, as St. Paul reminds us. We can develop a narcissistic overconcern with our bodies, or at the other end we can develop a contempt for them. A third option is to seek to glorify, to reveal God, in our bodies (1 Cor 6:20). Anything we feel or do with our bodies is a form of prayer when our central intent is opening to God's Presence through what we do.

In a sense, we can say that different dimensions of our bodies have their own way of praying. A woman once came up to me with an astonished look on her face after a period of praying with her hands raised and exclaimed, "My hands prayed!" It was, she realized, different from her mind praying. Our minds, bodies, and spirits form a unity in diversity, but our bodies have their own integrity in opening to God—an integrity that needs to be respected and given room.

Our bodily senses of taste, smell, touch, hearing, and sight can all be connected to our life in God. Each of them at a given time can be an avenue of grace, a way that we sense ourselves being drawn toward our ground in God. For example, I can sit before an icon of Christ and be given a sense of God's Spirit flooding through the icon's eyes with an opening love, or I can encounter a sunset, flower, or baby and sense divine Presence in its beauty. Each of our senses can also have ways of drawing us *away* from awareness of God. A particular person or object I see, for example, might invoke fear or numbness in me, or I might become overattracted and find myself completely displacing God with what I see.

Sometimes directees might be drawn to attend God's Presence in some new ways through their senses. The possibilities are manifold, including such things as sculpting with clay, sitting before an icon, and listening, playing, or moving to music. The whole embodied realm of the arts and imagination is brought into the sacred circle when it is approached with a desire for appreciating the divine. Celtic tradition speaks of our need to "tune the five-stringed harp" of our senses, to attune them to the divine Presence. Our senses are avenues for divine play, appreciation, and compassion in us. We may miss something of that divine vibrancy if we forget that each sense is connected not only to the creatures of God, but also to the One who gives the senses.

A spiritual director can be sensitive to how a directee is viewing the body and opening to the ways God's Spirit may be coming through different senses and other dimensions of the body, including perhaps through particular means of artistic expression. How is God appreciated in the life of the body? How is a directee called to express delight in its divine creation, to care for it, and to let its gestures, breath, postures, movements, senses, pain, and nourishment open into prayer?[12]

Sometimes the body's life can be brought to bear in the spiritual direction session itself. For example, if a directee comes to the session very exhausted or panicky, besides beginning the session with silence and prayer, the director might suggest a short breathing exercise, saying something like: "Let your breath slow down; keep your mind in the flow of your breathing; let everything else melt into your breath; just be present in simple trust of God's loving Presence, living right in the center of your moving breath."

The Director's Perennial First Task •

In the director's involvement with all of the communal icons of the spiritual life described in this chapter, the kinds of suggested questions and reflection given are secondary to the perennial first task of the director in listening to a directee: directly, immediately opening to God.

All our knowledge is meant to surround, not replace, this central humble opening in unknowing to the One who knows infinitely more than we and who we want to be the real Guide in this moment and all moments. Our own knowledge will most authentically come to bear in connection with this open leaning back into the abyss of Holy Wisdom.

CHAPTER 8

THE EVOLVING FUTURE
OF SPIRITUAL DIRECTION

Spiritual direction, like all ministries, is an opportunity to intentionally share the life of God among us. That life is dynamic, not static. Its forms and understandings will change in accordance with the ways we encounter the living Spirit of God. That encounter always contains a heart of mystery that we cannot fully understand. What we think is of the Spirit is easily mixed up with the movements of our ego fears and delusions. I think, however, that the Spirit is hidden even in these movements, ever at work through all that is, to reveal life whole in God.

I would like to sketch some of the spiritual direction trends and needs that I see on the horizon today. I offer these probes as opportunities for your reflection on the evolving future of this ministry. I hope they will stimulate you to add your own hunches and to think about some of their implications for your understanding and way of relating to this ministry.

Some Spiritual Direction Trends •

1. Proliferation of Programs

In 1978, when the Shalem Institute began its first spiritual direction program, there were only two other existing programs in the United States and none outside that I am aware of. By 1996 there were hundreds of such programs worldwide, mostly in North America. Most that I know of are short-term introductions to this ministry. A few of them are in-depth offerings with extensive requirements for admission and graduation, extending over a year or more. Sponsorship includes theological schools, university graduate schools, retreat centers, jurisdictional programs (dioceses, synods, etc.), and independent spiritual centers. Most of these programs are open to an ecumenical mix of participants, but the overwhelming preponderance of them are sponsored by Roman Catholic groups and many of the rest by Anglican/ Episcopalian ones, with the theological/ecclesial base of teaching often influenced by these particular traditions. In an era of great openness across denominational lines, especially in the area of spirituality, I think the conditioned theological differences among participants in programs are much less of a concern than they would have been in the past. In my experience I have sensed a great deal of respect for the denominational traditions of everyone. Indeed, I find many people wanting to stretch beyond their denominational boundaries to be enriched by others. A few programs have begun with broader ecumenical sponsorship.[1]

2. Broadening of Participation

In 1978 most formal spiritual direction was still being done by ordained clergy and members of religious communities, most of them Roman Catholic, along with some Anglicans and Eastern Orthodox. By 1995 I would guess that almost every Christian denomination had at least a few lay as well as clergy members offering some form of intentional spiritual companionship (even though many of those denominations do not officially recognize this ministry and its practice is still unusual among many of them). A growing number of Jewish rabbis and laypeople that I know of (apart from Hassidim, who have long revered the rabbi as a kind of spiritual director) have also come to value this ministry in a new way. Some of the inspiration for spiritual direction, I believe, has come not only from within Christian and Jewish traditions, but also from increasing exposure to Buddhist, Hindu, and Sufi-Moslem faiths, where a long-term experiential relationship with a spiritual elder is highly valued.

Among more evangelical denominations, classical spiritual direction overlaps with what some of them would call "shepherding" or "discipling," as I mentioned in chapter five. I would predict that more and more people in the huge Evangelical Christian community worldwide will discover and embrace elements of traditional spiritual direction in the years ahead. This ministry, I think, will be an avenue of spiritual "convergence" (not merger) between "mainstream" Christian and non-Fundamentalist Evangelical Protestant traditions. Some of the most popular books and periodicals among such Evangelicals have been very positively unearthing many practices of the larger Christian spiritual heritage, such as spiritual direction.

I would also predict that in a more subdued way spiritual direction will grow as an avenue of convergence between churched and unchurched individual seekers. Spiritual direction already serves as a kind of "halfway house" for a number of unchurched people who believe in God and are serious about their spiritual lives, but for various reasons cannot at the moment commit themselves fully to a formal Christian community.

Finally, I think that spiritual direction will continue to serve indirectly as a means of appreciating the spiritual experience and practices of other deep religious traditions. In direction one becomes used to dwelling on the edge of mystery, probing for the sacred truths and callings of our lives. It is a very different atmosphere than one where Christian doctrine is taught and boundaries are emphasized. Direction often enables us to touch a depth of relationship that is not fully capturable in theological language. We become freer to talk with (or read about) someone's experience from a different tradition at a level beneath the words. This doesn't mean that we will necessarily be strongly attracted to other traditions or see them as the same as our own, but we can find ourselves more open to the overlaps, challenged to go deeper, and respectful of the ineffable core of each deep tradition.

3. The Increase of Lay Directors

Probably thousands of new people every year are discovering the discipline and gift of spiritual direction, which in turn has led a growing number of people to sense a call to offer it as a ministry. The big news here, I think, is that more and more laypeople have sensed this call, especially laywomen. Since there are vastly more laypeople than ordained clergy and vowed members of religious communities, this trend has allowed far more people to have access to this ministry.

In the future I predict that the number of lay directors will continue to grow significantly, allowing this ministry to flourish far more than it ever has in history. This trend reflects the growing sense that the laity can share, in accord with their particular gifts, many kinds of spiritual ministry that once were thought to belong more exclusively to ordained clergy, especially in more hierarchical traditions. Theologically, baptism, rather than ordination or commitment to a vowed religious community, is being seen more and more as the primary ground of spiritual calling for all Christians, opening the potential for spiritual direction to everyone.

This trend toward lay directors moves spiritual direction back to its roots in the desert, where most of the spiritual fathers and mothers were not ordained clergy or parts of organized and sanctioned religious communities. Instead of laypeople withdrawn into the desert, though, today's lay spiritual directors are involved in every conceivable vocation.

Their increasing presence as directors has democratized this ministry. In many spiritual direction training programs, clergy, vowed religious, and laypeople are learning side by side as equals. What increasingly counts is not one's formal religious status but one's personal charism for this ministry. The past prevalent but confusing assumption that ordained and vowed religious had the charism of spiritual direction by virtue of their religious status, I think, is rapidly dying. This relieves such people without a real charism for direction not to feel they must force themselves to practice this ministry, and it frees those who really have such a gift to be recognized and encouraged.

The variety of backgrounds and spiritual sensitivities of these laypeople brings a great richness to this ministry. As spiritual direction spreads, it will encounter an increasing variety of cultural and religious backgrounds to which directors need to bring respect and sensitivity. Insofar as the director is given to God in prayer for the directee, I think there is an atmosphere that allows the Spirit to work directly in such sessions apart from the director's understanding of the directee's cultural and religious background. Thus a lack of full understanding need not be an impediment for a fruitful relationship. On the other hand, as implied in the section on pluralism in chapter seven, an awareness of the differences between director and directee can allow for more care in interpreting what is said in a session; also, a greater ease on the part of the directee is evident when an individual's differences are recognized and honored.

4. Pressure toward Professionalization

The proliferation of programs and numbers of directors has raised questions about standards of accountability, both for programs and for directors. In 1988 the first inclusive international (though mostly North American) gathering both for directors and for the staff of direction programs met at the Mercy Center in Burlingame, California. From that meeting a new organization came into being, Spiritual Directors International (SDI).[2] This organization holds two back-to-back meetings annually, one for the staffs of spiritual direction training/enrichment programs, and the other for spiritual directors in general. Besides giving an opportunity for lectures and workshops concerning the nature and practice of direction and training, these meetings have provided an ongoing forum for current issues relevant to spiritual direction, such as considering whether or not spiritual direction programs and directors should be accredited in some way and whether and what kind of ethical guidelines are needed.

These have proved to be controversial subjects. In chapter five I spelled out a range of possible ways of understanding the spiritual companion relationship. Members of SDI can be found at all points in this range, sometimes at multiple points. Let me summarize my own predilection, made clear in this book, with much of which I think a great many spiritual directors would agree:

I see spiritual direction primarily as a vocation to be given to the mystery of God's loving presence on behalf of another person, trusting that God's Spirit will guide this person in and beyond the director's presence and that discernment of this guidance may or may not be graced to come through the director as opposed to the directee. In either case, the discernment needs to be affirmed by the directee. In a given direction session the primary guidance of the Spirit may well show itself to be for the *director* through the directee.

Direction is primarily God's work in the presence of our desire for that work to proceed, work that is sometimes secret and sometimes manifest to our consciousness in the direction session. It is not primarily the work of the figuring-out mind of the director or the directee. The mind is a gifted vehicle of reflection on what it can perceive to be happening between God and us, but it has a tendency to go off on its own and lose its connectedness to the Spirit's immediate Presence. Thus it needs to lean back into that Presence again and again, touching into its true source of inspiration more directly. Our part in spiritual direction, I think, is mostly willingness and deep openness; everything of significant value for our minds comes from these qualities.

Some spiritual direction program staff would give more weight than I to the importance of the director's analytical skills and knowledge in the relationship, with a larger sense of the director's role and responsibility, as would be central to a professional counseling relationship. With such a view, there is sometimes a sense that professional standards of measurement for a qualified director are possible and needed, and that objective standards are needed for training programs, as well. Some such people, along with some church authorities, are concerned that without such standards for directors, everybody can assume the title of spiritual director, as well as define what they do as spiritual directors in their own various ways, sometimes to the confusion and detriment of the directee.

In a time when lawsuits for malfeasance in pastoral relationships of various kinds are rife, it is understandable that church officials especially would be tempted to try and control the practice of spiritual direction through strict guidelines and a desire for some kind of accreditation system. The great danger of trying to contain spiritual direction in these ways is that the primary historic test of this charism might be lost: that is, people spontaneously seek you out for help with their life in God because they sense God in you for them, regardless of your formal credentials.

While signs of malfeasance can often be apparent to everyone who hears about them, the positive essence of a gifted director is often less apparent. Ultimately, it can only be sensed by the person who seeks that person out as a director. The same person may not be sensed as a good director by someone else, since I don't believe the charism is an objective anointing of someone as a called director for anyone, but just for certain people. That is one more complicating factor in any attempt to develop a more standardized spiritual direction ministry.

Spiritual Directors International has developed a set of "Guidelines for Ethical Conduct" for spiritual directors. These outline concerns related to the spiritual director's own life, their relation to the directee, and to the larger community. If these are taken as a list of professional standards that adequately define this ministry, then I think they have tilted toward a professional model of spiritual direction. If they are taken as a means of "raising awareness among directors of certain problematic areas and offer practical parameters within which the charism God has entrusted to us may flourish," to quote one of the founders of SDI, Sister Mary Ann Scofield,[3] then I think they can have value for directors, especially if one selects those elements that are not influenced by a professional counseling model but by the integrity of the charism itself. In the end, each of us can only authentically embrace guidelines that honor our understanding of spiritual direction and support our freedom for God and our sense of accountability in its practice.

As for spiritual direction training/enrichment programs, these come from many theological, spiritual, and ecclesial standpoints and assumptions about the nature of spiritual direction, implicitly or explicitly. Perhaps what is most important is that these programs be as clear as possible to potential applicants about their assumptions, purposes, and methods, both concerning the nature of spiritual direction and of the program itself, so that people will be able to sense their own compatibility with them as much as possible before becoming committed to them. The variety of program emphases I predict will continue to be maintained in the future, and the richness of these differences can prove to be a good stimulus and challenge between programs.

As ethical guidelines and training programs become more prominent, let me hold up once again the need to respect the kind of informal and occasional spiritual companioning that happens apart from formalized and regular practice, which is mentioned on the spectrum of types of guidance relationships in chapter five. When this informal companioning is authentic, it is the result of the Spirit's bringing someone to a companion who, with or without any special preparation, has a true and gifted sense of accountability to be given to God for their neighbor as the other person speaks of God in their life.

I'm sure that an enormous amount of fine prayer, reflection, and discernment often happens in these encounters.

In all humility we need to remember that God's Spirit among us is a great mystery, blowing as it wills. We must leave room for the ways that Spirit moves between people that may confound many of our assumptions about who a "good" spiritual companion is, or even who is companioning whom at a given time. We dare not try to domesticate and monopolize the Holy Spirit's ways of being seen in reflective human relationships through overly confident and narrow assumptions about the nature of spiritual companioning (including any of my own such assumptions!).

Our attempts to enrich ourselves and others in the practice of this ministry are wonderful expressions of our concern for its being the best kind of companioning possible. But in the end, as scripture shows repeatedly, the Spirit chooses whom the Spirit will as a vessel of communication and reflection. Jesus, the uncredentialed country carpenter, is the chief exemplar of this freedom of the Spirit.

5. Spiritual Direction as Prophetic Probing Ground

To the extent that spiritual direction focuses on the Holy Spirit's direct presence and guidance, informed by our historical sacred stories and communities, I believe that this ministry expresses values that will continue to challenge any ecclesial, political, or social system that does not actively respect such a direct relationship of God with the individual. Though the ordering of church and society will involve different roles of authority and knowledge in order to function well, spiritual direction assumes an egalitarianism at the soul level, and by implication an equal valuing of everyone's human well-being, with all that this implies for the just structuring of human community. Everyone is born of God; God loves everyone equally; God is dynamically present for everyone equally, though in different forms and with different degrees of recognition and embracing at different periods of our lives.

This democratization of the Spirit gives enormous dignity to the individual. Every person is to be reverenced as an expression of divine grace. Human community, along with the community of creation, is also reverenced as the interwoven working ground of God's Spirit among us. Life at its spiritual heart becomes a trusting probe, a responsiveness *to* and a celebration *of* God's energy ever at work, shaping life into further marvelous being. This mysterious divine energy flares out into recognition among us in ever-surprising ways.

When we gather in a spiritual direction session we are called to recognize the holy ground upon which all life stands. Together we probe what God is growing in that ground. We seek for our unique place among the growing shoots of life we see. We listen for how the Spirit is loosening, planting, pruning, healing, and enjoying us. When we put our ear to this ground in direction, we are hearing something of God's work and delight not only in ourselves, but echoing in the rest of creation as well. We touch the ground that bore the prophecies of scripture, the revelation of divine love in Jesus Christ, and the divine intimacies and missions of the great saints. We stand on the meeting ground of heaven and earth, willingly exposed to the divine breath's murmurings. As this intent of spiritual direction becomes more widely recognized and tasted, this ministry will take an ever more appreciated place among spiritual practices as a vital seedbed of the Spirit, through which God's shalom on earth is given special growing room.

NOTES

CHAPTER 1

1. For a reflection on understandings of evil, see Barry Whitney, *What Are They Saying About God and Evil?* (Mahwah, N.J.: Paulist Press, 1989). He makes the valuable point that "Mystical confirmations of a loving Presence...reassure and console us that life indeed is good, despite the evil and suffering we must endure" (p. 91).

2. See John T. McNeill, *A History of the Cure of Souls* (New York: Harper and Row, 1951) for elaboration of Jewish, Greek, and Christian approaches.

3. See Louis Bouyer, *The Spirituality of the New Testament and the Fathers* (New York: Desclee, 1960), vol. 1, p. 31.

4. Aelred of Rievaulx, *On Spiritual Friendship* (Washington, D.C.: Consortium Press, 1974).

5. "Aelred in the Tradition of Monastic Friendship," ibid., p. 36ff.

6. Thanks to Athanasius's *The Life of St. Antony,* Ancient Christian Writers series (Westminster, Md.: Newman, 1950).

7. Ibid., p. 25ff.

8. Irenee Hausherr, S.J., *Spiritual Direction in the Early Christian East* (Kalamazoo, Mich.: Cistercian Publications, 1990).

9. Thomas Merton, "The Spiritual Father in the Desert Tradition," *Contemplation in a World of Action* (New York: Doubleday, 1965), p. 281f. For further exploration of the desert tradition, see Merton, *Wisdom of the Desert* (New York: New Directions, 1960); Helen Waddell, *The Desert Fathers* (Ann Arbor: Univ. of Michigan Press, 1972); Benedicta Ward, *Sayings of the Desert Fathers* (Oxford: Mowbrays, 1975); John Cassian, *Confer-*

ences, Classics of Western Spirituality (Mahwah, N.J.: Paulist Press, 1985).

10. See Catherine de Hueck Doherty, *Poustinia* (Notre Dame, Ind.: Ave Maria Press, 1975).

11. See Bouyer, p. 307f.

12. Quoted by P. A. Sorokin in *The Ways and the Power of Love* (Boston: Beacon Press, 1954), in the chapter, "Monastic Psychoanalysis, Counseling, and Therapy."

13. Thomas Merton, *Contemplation in a World of Action* (New York: Doubleday, 1971), p. 269.

14. See Gerald May, *Care of Mind, Care of Spirit* (New York: Harper and Row, 1982) for an excellent and practical discussion of the relation of psychological and spiritual reality, and of the psychiatric dimensions of spiritual direction.

15. See Bernard Tickerhoof, *Conversion and the Enneagram* (Denville, N.J.: Dimension Books, 1991) and James Empereur, *The Enneagram and Spiritual Direction* (New York: Continuum, 1997) as two among many resources for understanding the Enneagram in a Christian context.

CHAPTER 2

1. See Jeffrey Boyd, *Reclaiming the Soul* (Cleveland: Pilgrim Press, 1996) for a refutation of this fear.

2. Quoted in Eric Klein and John P. Izzo, *The Corporate Soul.* (Brielle, N.J.: TradeWinds Press, 1998).

3. For an elaboration of biblical understanding see "Soul" in William Gentz, ed., *The Dictionary of Bible and Religion* (Nashville: Abingdon, 1986) and *The Interpreter's Dictionary of the Bible* (Nashville: Abingdon, 1962), vol. 4.

4. Thomas Merton. *Conjectures of a Guilty Bystander* (New York: Doubleday, 1966), p. 142.

5. Raymond Blakney, *Meister Eckhart: A Modern Translation* (New York: Harper and Row, 1941), p. 129.

6. John Moyne and Coleman Barks, *Open Secret: Versions of Rumi* (Putney, Vt.: Threshold Press, 1984).

7. Daniel Helminiak, *The Human Core of Spirituality: Mind as Psyche and Spirit* (Albany: State University of New York Press, 1996). I believe this book is an important contribution to a contemporary understanding of the relation of mind, body, and spirit. The theologian Bernard Lonergan is a major influence.

8. See Barry Whitney, *What Are They Saying About God and Evil?* (Mahwah, N.J.: Paulist Press, 1989) for different understandings of evil. At one point the author says, "Mystical confirmations of a loving Presence...reassure and console us that life indeed is good, despite the evil and suffering we must endure" (p. 91).

CHAPTER 3

1. For example, see Tarthang Tulku, *Time, Space, and Knowledge* (Emeryville, Calif.: Dharma Publications, 1977).

2. For the sake of greater precision it might be helpful to offer one way of defining spirituality and theology at this point. *Spirituality* in a general sense refers to our probing and responses to the basic mysterious human yearning for the infinite. It is that underlying dimension of consciousness that openly waits and searches for a transcendent fulfillment of our human nature. *Christian* spirituality involves such probing and response in the context of historical and contemporary Christian experience, faith, and community. It can take many forms, but it always takes seriously an intrinsic love of God for creation and a wounded yet partially free human nature that in God's Spirit in Christ is called and empowered toward conversion, i.e., toward ever deeper sight and life in the image of God.

Spiritual theology at its purest could be said to involve images and thoughts that arise from our prayerful presence and are directly aimed at feeding our own and others' relationships with God. Other forms of theology operate at a more generalized cognitive level of interpretation and integration, providing a broad context for looking at our experience. Recently theology has been recognizing spirituality more fully in its explorations. As a result, the relationship between theology and spirituality is in flux today. Theology perhaps is coming to realize more fully its own spiritual core.

For an insightful description of the evolving relationship of spirituality and theology, see Philip Sheldrake, "The Study of Spirituality," in *The Way* 39, no. 2 (April 1999).

3. For a helpful interpretation of the complementarity of the apophatic and kataphatic ways, see Harvey Egan, "Christian Apophatic and Kataphatic Mysticisms," *Theological Studies* (Fall 1978).

4. See Innocentia Richards, trans., "Discernment of Spirits," from the *Dictionnaire de Spiritualité: Ascetique et Mystique,* vol. 3 (Collegeville, Minn.: Liturgical Press, 1970).

5. See "Discernment of Spirits," op. cit., for a helpful interpretation of such scriptural bases.

6. Louis Puhl, *The Spiritual Exercises of Ignatius Loyola* (Chicago: Loyola University Press, 1951), p. 84ff.

7. See (in addition to notes 4 and 6) such resources as Maureen Conroy, *The Discerning Heart: Discerning a Personal God* (Chicago: Loyola University Press, 1993); Suzanne Farnham, et al. *Listening Hearts* (Harrisburg, Pa.: Morehouse Publishing, 1991); Thomas Green, *Weeds Among the Wheat* (Notre Dame, Ind.: Ave Maria Press, 1984); John English, *Choosing Life* (New York: Paulist Press, 1978); Dorothy Bass ed., *Practicing Our Faith* (San Francisco: Jossey-Bass, 1998); and the monthly periodical *Review for Religious.*

8. Compare, for example, Ignatius or any of his interpreters with any writing of Archbishop Anthony Bloom or Kallistos Ware (e.g., "The Spiritual Father in Orthodox Christianity," in *Cross Currents* 24, nos. 2–3 (Summer-Fall 1974).

9. Probably the most thorough and inclusive discussion of Quaker practices is in a three-volume series by Patricia Loring, all under the title *Listening Spirituality.* The first volume deals with individual practices, the second with communal practices, and the third (not yet available as of this writing), with the Quaker social witness. The first volume is from a private press, Openings Press. This series is privately published (vol. 1 in 1997, vol. 2 in 1999) and is probably most easily available through the Friends General Con-

ference Bookstore (Philadelphia); phone: 800-966-4556, e-mail: <bookstore@fgc.quaker.org>. Also see Michael Sheeran, *Beyond Majority Rule* (Philadelphia: Philadelphia Yearly Meeting, 1996).

10. Denis Edwards, *Human Experience of God* (Mahwah, N.J.: Paulist Press, 1983), p. 117.

11. *The Ascent of Mount Carmel* 2:16.6–7, found in Kieran Kavanaugh and Otilio Rodriguez, trans., *The Collected Works of St. John of the Cross* (Washington, D.C.: Institute of Carmelite Studies, 1979), pp.152–53.

12. Denis Edwards, op. cit., pp. 126–27. This entire small volume provides an excellent discussion of the experience of God in a Christian context, including a very concise, practical chapter on "Finding God's Will." For help concerning the psychological and spiritual dimensions of experience, see Gerald May, *Care of Mind, Care of Spirit.*

13. G. R. Evans, trans., *Bernard of Clairvaux: Selected Works* (Mahwah, N.J.: Paulist Press, 1987).

14. For his lengthy and profound commentary on the dark night, see John of the Cross, *Ascent of Mount Carmel* (in his *Collected Works,* previously cited).

CHAPTER 4

1. Another way of looking at spiritual paths is found in the "Creation Spirituality" schema found in many of the works of Matthew Fox.

2. As examples of many books available on spiritual practices, see my *Living in the Presence* (Harper San Francisco, 1995); Dorothy Bass, ed., *Practicing Our Faith: A Way of Life for a Searching People* (San Francisco: Jossey-Bass, 1998); Marjorie Thompson, *Soul Feast: An Invitation to Christian Spiritual Life* (Louisville, Ky.: Westminster John Knox Press, 1995); Richard Foster, *Celebration of Discipline* (Harper San Francisco, 1978).

3. See Tilden Edwards, *Sabbath Time* (Nashville: Upper Room, 1992).

4. See Craig Mueller, "Dreams and Spiritual Direction," *Presence* 4, no. 3 (Sept. 1998).

5. For further reading about journal keeping, see Anne Broyles, *Journaling: A Spirit Journey* (Nashville: Upper Room, 1988); Morton Kelsey, *Adventure Inward* (Minneapolis: Augsburg, 1980); Ira Progoff, *At a Journal Workshop* (New York: Dialogue House Library, 1980).

6. Kieran Kavanaugh and Otilio Rodriguez, trans. *The Collective Works of St. John of the Cross* (Washington, D.C.: ICS Publications, 1979). See paragraphs 17–67 (p. 620 ff.) of the commentary on the third stanza of *The Living Flame of Love* for John's views of spiritual direction. For his view of the delicate transition time between meditative and contemplative prayer in a person's life, which he believes requires special vigilance on the part of the director, see *The Ascent of Mount Carmel II:* 13, 2–4, and *The Dark Night I:* 9, 2–8.

CHAPTER 5

1. Thomas Merton, "The Spiritual Father in the Desert Tradition," *Contemplation in a World of Action* (N.Y.: Doubleday, 1965), pp. 271, 286. For John of the Cross's own words, see his *Ascent of Mount Carmel II:*13, 2–4, and *The Dark Night I:* 9, 2–8, in John's previously cited *Collected Works.*

2. See footnote 6, chapter 4.

3. See Kieran Kavanaugh and Otilio Rodriguez, trans., *Saint Teresa of Avila: Collected Works,* vol. 1 (Washington, D.C.: Institute for Carmelite Studies, 1987), especially pp. 130–31.

4. Cited by Joseph de Guibert, *The Theology of the Spiritual Life,* pp. 100, 155.

5. See the works of such writers as Jean La Place, Norbert Brockman, Adrian Van Kaam, and Vilma Seelaus. See also the authors in the bibliography, appendix C.

6. Thomas Merton, "Spiritual Direction," *Sponsa Regis,* vol. 30 (1958–59).

7. Gerald May wrote an article for the *Shalem News* (Winter 1998) entitled "Varieties of Spiritual Companionship," which helped to inspire this listing, but that article deserves to be read

in its own integrity, since I have provided a different version out of my own experience.

8. An extension program for facilitators of group spiritual direction is available at the Shalem Institute.

CHAPTER 6

1. The discussion of boundaries is adopted from a speech given by me to the annual meeting of Spiritual Directors International and later published in 1994 in SDI's periodical, *Presence* (vol.1, no. 2) under the title, "Immediate Givenness to God in the Spiritual Direction Relationship."

2. For discussion of these stages, see such works as James Fowler, *Faith Development and Pastoral Care* (Philadelphia: Fortress Press, 1987) and *Stages of Faith* (San Francisco: Harper and Row, 1981); Gabriel Moran, *Religious Education Development* (Indianapolis: Winston Press, 1983); and Evelyn Underhill's classic, *Mysticism* (New York: Meridian, 1974).

CHAPTER 7

1. For further examination of the complexities of men and women related to spiritual development in a Christian context, one resource is Stephen B. Clark, *Man and Woman in Christ: An Examination of the Roles of Men and Women in Light of Scripture and the Social Sciences* (Ann Arbor, Mich.: Servant Books, 1980). A recent helpful article related to men is: Dom Violi and Marie Joyce, "Searching for Masculine Identity," in *The Way* (Fall 1998).

2. See, for example, Elizabeth Johnson, *She Who Is* (New York: Crossroad, 1994); Ann Carr, *Transforming Grace: Christian Tradition and Women's Experience* (San Francisco: Harper and Row, 1988); Joann Wolski Conn, ed., *Women's Spirituality: Resources for Christian Development* (Mahwah, N.J.: Paulist Press, 1986).

3. For further consideration of this area, see Robert Annechino, "Bridegroom Mysticism" (*Review for Religious*, December 1991).

4. For a view of people with alternative sexual orientations in spiritual direction, and an extensive bibliography, see Peg Thompson, "The Coming Out Process in Spiritual Direction," *Presence*, vol. 4, no. 3 (Sept. 1998). For a more comprehensive treatment see James Empereur, *Spiritual Direction and the Gay Person* (New York: Continuum, 1999).

5. An increasing number of books related to spirituality and the workplace are available. Here are a few examples: Matthew Fox, *The Reinvention of Work: A New Vision of Livelihood for Our Time* (San Francisco: Harper Collins, 1994); Parker Palmer, *The Active Life: A Spirituality of Work, Creativity, and Caring* (New York: Harper and Row, 1990); John Haughey, *Converting 9 to 5: A Spirituality of Daily Work* (New York: Crossroad, 1989); Nancy Eggert, *Contemplative Leadership for Entrepreneurial Organizations* (Westport, Conn.: Quorum, 1998). The Shalem Institute has been exploring the area of the workplace, spirituality, and leadership through its "Soul of the Executive" extension program.

6. See Robert Duggan, "Liturgical Spirituality and Liturgical Reform," in *Spiritual Life* (Spring 1981) for a helpful review of the place of liturgy in the spiritual life.

7. See John Haughey, *The Holy Use of Money* (New York: Doubleday, 1986) for a scripturally based understanding of the power and use of money.

8. For further consideration of spiritual direction in a cross-cultural perspective, see Susan Rakoczy, ed., *Common Journey, Different Paths: Spiritual Direction in Cross-Cultural Perspective* (Maryknoll, N.Y.: Orbis, 1992).

9. For reading in the area of interfaith spirituality, see such works as: Lavinia Byrne, ed., *Traditions of Spiritual Guidance* (Collegeville, Minn.: Liturgical Press, 1990); Beatrice Bruteau, *What We Can Learn from the East* (New York: Crossroad, 1995); Arthur Green, ed., *Jewish Spirituality* (New York: Crossroad, 1989, vol. 1; 1994, vol. 2); Susan Walker, ed., *Speaking of Silence: Christians and Buddhists on the Contemplative Way* (Mahwah, N.J.: Paulist Press, 1987); Seyyed Hossein Nasr, ed., *Islamic Spirituality,* (New York: Crossroad, 1987); John Sommerfeldt, ed., *Abba: Guides to Wholeness and*

Holiness East and West (Kalamazoo, Mich.: Cistercian Publications, 1982); and any books by Raimon Pannikar.

10. Some of these questions are inspired by Segundo Galilea in "Liberation as an Encounter with Politics and Contemplation," *Concilium 96*. The last question is from Shaun McCarty, S.T., a former staff member of the Shalem Spiritual Guidance Program. For a more specific and comprehensive way to help a directee with understanding and discernment related to a call in the social arena, see Elinor Shea, "Spiritual Direction and Social Consciousness," *The Way Supplement* 54 (Autumn 1985).

11. Some spiritually oriented ecology readings include: Jay McDaniel, *With Roots and Wings* (New York: Orbis Books, 1995); Charles Cummings, *Ecospirituality: Toward a Reverent Life* (Mahwah, N.J.: Paulist Press, 1991); A. J. Fritsch, *Down to Earth Spirituality* (Kansas City: Sheed and Ward, 1992); Stephen Scharper and Hilary Cunningham, *The Green Bible* (New York: Orbis Books, 1993).

12. See Tilden Edwards, *Living in the Presence* (San Francisco: Harper Collins, revised version 1995), chapter two, for further ways of understanding and attending the body as part of the spiritual life. Also see *Weavings* 14, no.4 (July/August 1999): all of the articles in this issue are dedicated to spirituality and the body.

CHAPTER 8

1. For a more detailed summary and suggested criteria for evaluation of spiritual direction programs, see Janet K. Ruffing, "Look at Every Path Closely and Deliberately: What's on Offer?" *The Way Supplement,* 1995/84.

2. Any spiritual director is eligible for membership in SDI. For further information, contact the organization at 1329 Seventh Ave., San Francisco, Calif., 94122-2507; E-mail: presence@ sdiworld.org; Tel.: (415) 566-1560; Fax: (415) 566-1277; Web site: http://www.sdiworld.org.

3. Quoted in *Connections*, the newsletter of SDI, vol. 8, no.1 (March 1999).

APPENDIX A

WHERE CAN WE FIND FURTHER HELP?

The first place to turn for help, both in our own spiritual lives and as directors, is always inward, not outward—turning to our deep soul in God with our hope that the Spirit will show us what we need to see and do. We can bring that centeredness on God to scripture, as the desert fathers and mothers did, and pray to be shown what we need through the scriptural words. From there we can move to the help of Spirit-seeking people: our spiritual director, director peer groups, spiritual community, and authors of spiritual tapes and books.

We also might want to join Spiritual Directors International (mentioned in the last chapter), a grassroots organization of spiritual directors who hold an annual national workshop, as well as many periodic regional meetings. SDI is publisher of *Presence*, a periodical especially for spiritual directors that includes various articles on spiritual direction, training, supervision, and cultural contexts.

We may reach a point where we feel the need for a disciplined and extensive period of time dedicated to learning about spiritual direction more fully with others. No program can "make" us spiritual directors. As this book has tried to make clear, spiritual direction at its heart is a calling and a gift. But a good program, like an art school, can help to refine, test, and give perspective to the gift.

The number of formal programs related to spiritual direction has grown tremendously in recent years, as I mentioned in the last chapter. In looking at possible programs you should consider such factors as:

1. its compatibility with your understanding of spiritual life and direction;

2. the experience and emphases of the staff and their respect for individual differences;

3. the location and kinds of prayer offered;

4. academic versus experiential emphases;

5. denominational versus ecumenical emphasis in its theological grounding and practice;

6. the amount of requirements, time, and type of structure involved;

7. the kind of spirituality emphasized by the staff;

8. the kinds of participants that have been attracted, including their faith traditions, vocational spread, and experience with spiritual direction.

You may want to talk with several graduates of the program to get their views of its strengths and limitations.

Shalem's Extension Program for Spiritual Directors •

I will briefly describe Shalem's program as an example of a particularly contemplative and ecumenically oriented approach. It is one of the oldest spiritual direction programs in the United States, having begun in 1978 with a grant awarded through the Association of Theological

Schools. Graduate credit for those who need it is available through the Washington Theological Union. The average class of about thirty lay, religious, and ordained people is drawn from all over North America and sometimes other countries. Participants usually represent about nine different denominational backgrounds.

Two eighteen-month classes begin each year, one with ten-day residencies a year apart in the winter, the other with residencies in the summer, in a retreat center near Baltimore. Every participant needs to show signs of a call to spiritual direction, especially that others come to them to talk about God in their lives, however informally this may be. At least two monthly relationships with directees must be formalized before entering. Also, a monthly peer group with a few other directors in one's locale needs to be formed or joined (see appendix B for an outline of the peer group process).

Every participant has some further personal experience with a spiritual director and feels a sense of call, or at least wanting to test a serious call, to this kind of ministry. Some participants have a great deal of experience as formal or informal spiritual companions, others relatively little. All share a personal desire for a truly God-centered and reflective life. The required readings, brief practical papers, peer groups, seminars, spiritual direction, self-selected prayer practices, and residential gatherings all assume an invitation to further personal spiritual deepening as the ground for being a mature spiritual companion for someone.

Direction at Shalem is not approached as an objective skill, but as a gifted spinoff of a discerning, God-desiring life. The desert fathers and mothers are our exemplars to the extent that they did not train those who came seeking God to be spiritual directors. From what we know they offered simple but stretching practices and words of spiritual wisdom tailored to what they intuited as the seeker's spiritual needs at a given time. The seeker learned most from the pioneering intimacy of the abba/amma with God. They wanted to share that intimacy. In time, as the seeker's own intimacy with God matured, they might become an abba or amma for others. Seekers did not come to the abba or amma to *become* one, though. They came to realize their life in God more deeply with the help of their mentor.

The lay, religious, and clergy staff members of Shalem's program certainly are not abbas and ammas, but each one values their firsthand experience and the experience of the tradition with divine reality. This is what each most brings to the program, as this is translated into particular practical themes related to spiritual direction. Whatever we do with participants, we want as much as possible for it to be a three-way affair in every moment. We want God's Spirit to affect what we say and how we are heard in the moment of presentation. We want God's intimacy to show itself with us in those times. We want God's wisdom to astound us and bring us and the participants beyond what we thought when we prepared something for a program session. We want head and heart to remain united and open to the One who lives in us through every moment.

Given these motivations, we have not felt that *training* is the appropriate word for what we are doing with people. We have usually shied away from that term and spoken of an *enrichment* program. I doubt that we can really *train* a spiritual director any more than an early desert mother or father could. But we can stoke our students' desire for fullness and authenticity of life in God for themselves and their directees. We can expose and probe with them what we and others have learned about life in the Spirit, alone and with directees.

When our students are with directees, I think what they have going for them most is their own desire for intimacy with God, along with their desire for sensitivity to God's way with this unique person before them, in this new moment of time that they share together. I think they will be doing their best as directors when they can trust the fresh possibilities of God that show themselves in the spiritual direction session.

This trust is *surrounded* with whatever participants have learned about the spiritual life and direction. This knowledge, as earlier mentioned in this book, is not meant to be at the center of their consciousness. That sacred center is reserved for a childlike innocence desiring whatever is of God for the directee. Our program tries to cultivate this stance by mingling prayerfulness and reflection, trying never to let these drift too far apart from one another. This advocacy of the head in the spiritual heart allows divine-human intimacy to be more naturally sustained through the sessions of our program and models something of the stance of a director with a directee.

More specifically, the residencies of the program maintain a semi-retreat atmosphere. Seminars, prayer sessions, and spiritual direction peer groups weave themselves together, along with a thirty-six-hour guided period of silence in the middle of each residency, and some daily free time. I think what often happens best in these residencies are the spontaneous occasions of intimacy and insight that occur between individuals with God and among one another, sometimes leading to a transformed sense of reality. The program provides space and the background mantra of talks and practices; God then provides the only really worthwhile "training" for the participants as directors in the ways that only God knows the person needs.

This I think says something about the spiritual direction relationship itself. We find a promising relationship when the director is prayerfully present to God for directees, passionately desiring what God wants, but willing not to know what that is. The director gives protected, cared-for space for the unfolding of the directee's deep soul, rather than for the controlling, constricted, problem-solving level of their egos.

An additional extension program more narrowly focused on facilitating spiritual direction in *groups* has recently been added to Shalem's offerings.

Further information about Shalem's extension programs is available from the Shalem Institute office, web site, and e-mail:

> 5430 Grosvenor Lane
> Bethesda, Md. 20814
> (301) 897-7334
> Web Site: www.shalem.org
> E-mail: info@shalem.org

APPENDIX B

THE SPIRITUAL DIRECTOR PEER GROUP MEETING

The form of supervision chosen by a director needs to reflect one's understanding of spiritual direction and sense of its practice. The following model, honed over many years, has served Shalem spiritual direction program associates well.

This model assumes a monthly two-hour meeting. The ideal group would consist of about six practicing spiritual directors from a variety of backgrounds, who themselves have spiritual directors, are willing to commit themselves to meeting monthly, and to abide by the intents of the group. The initial meeting can include time for personal faith-sharing among the members, sharing of expectations and concerns, and corporate prayer. After the initial meeting, two members of the group present themselves in relation to a particular directee at each monthly session. The members rotate the role of convener; this should be a different person at a given meeting than either of the presenters.

Outline of Basic Intent, Focus, and Standards for Presentation and Reflection:

1. Seek spacious discernment of the Holy Spirit's presence rather than striving for problem solving.

2. Focus on the presenter rather than the directee, offering feedback, affirmation, questions, and insights that will assist the presenter's prayerful discernment about the relationship, including how the prayer experience and faith of the presenter is impinging upon and being affected by the relationships with the directee.

3. Remember that this is to be spiritual direction for the presenter.

4. Presenters: present *yourself* in relation to a directee, not the directee in relation to yourself. The presentation can include a specific incident in a direction session, a description of the relationship as it has developed over time, a brief account of a moment that seemed especially graced or problematic, or a follow-up of a relationship previously presented.

5. Be willing to call the group to silence if it is perceived that the group has lost its prayerful openness and drifted too far into problem solving or analysis.

6. Preserve the anonymity of the directee.

7. Keep peer group material confidential (within the group).

Outline of a Session •

1. Opening by convener:

   a. Remind the group of the meeting's intent and focus.

   b. Lead the group in silence, with or without spoken prayer or scripture (5 minutes).

2. First presentation (up to 15 minutes).

3. Brief questions for clarification only (1–2 minutes).

4. Silent, prayerful reflection and note taking (2–3 minutes).

5. Discussion (up to 35 minutes).

6. Break (5 minutes).

7. Second presentation (up to 15 minutes).

8. Brief questions for clarification only (1–2 minutes).

9. Silent, prayerful reflection and writing (2–3 minutes).

10. Discussion (up to 35 minutes).

11. Process of the meeting (5 minutes) led by convener: How well did we focus on the presenter (as opposed to the directee)? Did the group feel as though spiritual direction took place? Where did we get off track (e.g., not attentive to the Spirit, too much problem solving, overly analytical)? What was the quality of silence and attentiveness to God in the group? Was there any time when we sensed ourselves usurping the presenter's responsibility for discernment, as opposed to offering insights or questions that might assist the discernment of the presenter?

12. Closing silence led by convener, with or without spoken prayer (2–5 minutes).

APPENDIX C

SELECTED BIBLIOGRAPHY

An explosion of books and articles has appeared in the last several decades related to the history and practice of Christian spirituality and that of other religious traditions as well. This bibliography will be restricted to a selection of books that are directly related to the practice of spiritual direction.

The periodical published by Spiritual Directors International, *Presence*, is devoted exclusively to articles related to spiritual direction. Other periodicals that occasionally include articles relevant to spiritual direction include: *Review for Religious, Spiritual Life, Weavings,* and the British quarterly, *The Way.* The Shalem Institute's quarterly *Newsletter* often includes articles related to spiritual direction. These can be found on Shalem's web site (www.Shalem.org). The web site also provides links to lists of spirituality books, especially those grounded in mystical/contemplative tradition.

Addison, Howard. *Show Me Your Way.* Woodstock, Vt.: Skylight Path Publications, 2000.

Aelred of Rievaulx. *On Spiritual Friendship.* Kalamazoo, Mich.: Cistercian Publications, 1977.

Bakke, Jeannette. *Holy Invitations: Discovering Spiritual Direction.* Grand Rapids: Baker Books, 2000.

Ball, Peter. *Anglican Spiritual Direction.* Boston: Cowley Publications, 1998.

Barry, William, and William Connolly. *The Practice of Spiritual Direction.* New York: Seabury, 1982.

Buber, Martin. *Tales of the Hasidim.* New York: Schocken Books, 1947.

Byrne, Lavinia, ed. *Traditions of Spiritual Guidance.* Collegeville, Minn.: Liturgical Press, 1990.

Carroll, L. P., and K. M. Dyckman. *Inviting the Mystic, Supporting the Prophet.* Mahwah, N.J.: Paulist Press, 1982.

Chapman, Dom John. *Spiritual Letters.* New York: Sheed and Ward, 1969.

Conroy, Maureen. *The Discerning Heart: Discerning a Personal God.* Chicago: Loyola University Press, 1993.

Culligan, Kevin. *Spiritual Direction: Contemporary Readings.* New York: Living Flame Press, 1983.

Dougherty, Rose Mary. *Group Spiritual Direction: Community for Discernment.* Mahwah, N.J.: Paulist Press, 1995. Videotape also available through Paulist Press.

Edwards, Tilden. *Spiritual Friend.* Mahwah, NJ: Paulist Press, 1980.

Farnham, Suzanne. *Listening Hearts.* Harrisburg, Pa.: Morehouse Publications, 1991.

Francis de Sales and Jane de Chantal. *Letters of Spiritual Direction*. Peronne Marie Thibert, trans. Mahwah, N.J.: Paulist Press, 1988.

Gratton, Carolyn. *The Art of Spiritual Guidance*. New York: Crossroad, 1992.

Green, Thomas. *Weeds Among the Wheat*. Notre Dame, Ind.: Ave Maria Press, 1984.

Guenther, Margaret. *Holy Listening: The Art of Spiritual Direction*. Cambridge, Mass.: Cowley Publications, 1992.

Hart, Thomas. *The Art of Christian Listening*. Mahwah, N.J.: Paulist Press, 1980.

John of the Cross. *The Collected Works of John of the Cross*. Kieran Kavanaugh and Otilio Rodriguez, trans. Washington, D.C.: Institute of Carmelite Studies, 1990.

Jones, Alan. *Exploring Spiritual Direction*. Boston: Cowley Publications, 1982, 1999.

Kelsey, Morton. *Companions on the Inner Way*. New York: Crossroad, 1983.

Leech, Kenneth. *Soul Friend*. Harper San Francisco, 1980.

Liebert, Elizabeth. *Changing Life Patterns: Adult Development in Spiritual Direction*. Mahwah, N.J.: Paulist Press, 1992.

Luther, Martin. *Letters of Spiritual Counsel*. Theodore Tappert, ed. Philadelphia: Westminster Press, 1955.

May, Gerald. *Care of Mind/Care of Spirit: Psychiatric Dimensions of Spiritual Guidance*. Harper San Francisco, 1992.

McNeill, John. *A History of the Care of Souls.* New York: Harper and Row, 1977.

Merton, Thomas. *Spiritual Direction and Meditation.* Collegeville, Minn.: Liturgical Press, 1960.

Morris, Danny, and Charles Olsen. *Discerning God's Will Together.* Nashville: Upper Room, 1997.

Nemeck, F. K., and M. T. Coombs. *The Way of Spiritual Direction.* Wilmington, Del.: Michael Glazier Press, 1985.

Neufelder, Jerome, and Mary Coelho, eds. *Writings on Spiritual Direction.* New York: Seabury Press, 1982.

Ruffing, Janet. *Spiritual Direction: Beyond the Beginnings.* Mahwah, N.J.: Paulist Press, 2000.

Schimmel, Annemarie. *Mystical Dimensions of Islam.* Chapel Hill: University of North Carolina Press, 1975.

Sellner, Edward. *Mentoring: The Ministry of Spiritual Kinship.* Notre Dame, Ind.: Ave Maria Press, 1990.

Sheeran, Michael. *Beyond Majority Rule.* Philadelphia: Philadelphia Yearly Meeting, 1983.

Sommerfeldt, John, ed. *Abba: Guides to Wholeness and Holiness East and West.* Kalamazoo, Mich.: Cistercian Publications, 1982.

Steere, Douglas. *Friedrich von Hugel, Spiritual Counsel and Letters.* New York: Harper and Row, 1964.

Studzinski, Raymond. *Spiritual Direction and Mid-Life Development.* Chicago: Loyola University Press, 1985.

Sudbrack, Joseph. *Spiritual Guidance.* Mahwah, N.J.: Paulist Press, 1983.

Sullivan, John, ed. *Spiritual Direction.* Washington, D.C.: Institute of Carmelite Studies, 1980.

Teresa of Avila. *The Collected Works of Teresa of Avila.* Kieran Kavanaugh and Otilio Rodriguez, trans. Washington, D.C.: Institute of Carmelite Studies, 1980.

Underhill, Evelyn. *Letters.* Westminster, Md.: Christian Classics, 1989.

Ward, Benedicta, trans. *The Desert Christian: Sayings of the Desert Fathers.* New York: Macmillan, 1975.